Prais

M000289923

Up from the ASHES

Dinah Hodgson takes readers on a quest to explore themselves by sharing openly the journey from broken to whole of her own experience. From the pain and trauma that created a lost child, to the emergence of a mature leader of faith, Hodgson paints a picture of hope found in God for those still on the path of healing. Through this depth of experience, she helps her readers identify where they, too, are in captivity, exposing lies and strongholds that all too often are left unquestioned. Dinah beautifully demonstrates God's redemption in action, a beacon of light for citizens of our beautiful but broken world.

—Engela Hepworth, therapist, LMSW

Down to earth and authentic, *Up from the Ashes* gives victims of abuse a safe place to come and be heard. As Dinah shares her healing journey, you feel like you're sitting with her on her living room couch, just the two of you, talking about the real stuff of life, both the ugly and the beautiful. No true journey to freedom and healing in Christ is ever easy—the pain of discovery and confession always precedes God's overwhelming peace and restoration that follows. Dinah helps her readers confront that pain little by little, with compassion and confidence to the end.

—J. A. Marx, biblical counselor with Gateway Church
Author of *The Silenced Christian Wife: Validating, Encouraging, and Empowering Women in the Unspeakable Marital Crisis*

Dinah Hodgson engages her readers by weaving her restorative story into biblical principles, providing a credible foundation of theological perspectives on wholeness. Add this book to your spiritual formation library with a readiness to share with those seeking a better outcome of the confusion of their own life journey.

—Dr. Marion Ingegneri, MA, ThD (h.c.)
Founder and director, Women in Ministry Leadership Cohort, Phoenix, AZ

Up from the Ashes is rooted in the reality that Jesus desires all of us to walk free from the stuck places of our soul! While drawing on her own story, Dinah Hodgson grounds what she shares in Scripture, while providing her readers a practical pathway for real transformation. Walking alongside Dinah over the last three decades, I've experienced firsthand what Jesus has done both in and through her life. Now you have the opportunity to learn from her journey so you can lean into your own freedom.

—Dave Buehring
Founder and president of Lionshare

Dinah Hodgson offers a vulnerable window into the difficult realities of her childhood and explores how God's incredible redeeming power has been visible throughout her life. *Up from the Ashes* is a reminder to us all that broken foundations can be rebuilt through God. If you're working to process past hurts or are asking Jesus to reveal your next step in life, this is a must-read.

—Dr. Rob Hoskins
President, One Hope Pompano Beach, FL

Pastor Dinah Hodgson's ministry and life model how to walk out principles of finding freedom, restore identity in Christ, and walk in God's purpose and original design. Reading her story left me inspired and committed to work through deeper issues in my own heart. She shares her journey with both vulnerability and courage, which becomes an invitation to readers to find healing and freedom themselves.

—Jeff Gilliland, associate pastor and worship leader at
River of Life Community Church in Hudson, OH

Have you ever wondered what path someone took to get where they are? How do some emerge with a quiet confidence while others are gripped with fear? Dinah Hodgson's openness and honesty grabs you from the first pages, and the reveal of how her life was spiritually recaptured to impact the darkest facets of her life is encouraging. As the reader you are transported into her deeply difficult and heartbreaking moments that are eventually morphed into daily, practical living with joy from Almighty God. It's a must-read book that you'll be rereading and recommending to others.

—Laurie Frey, author and live entertainment producer

Not only is Dinah's story powerful in its honest vulnerability, but it is also crammed full of valuable insights and effective tools that she herself has discovered and used on her own journey to freedom. Her life speaks volumes, and her words are destined to become a beacon of hope to many who may find themselves in similar places of disfunction and despair.

—Helen Spicer, founding pastor of Mosaic Church Coventry
Founder and director of Cherished Hearts, UK

The revelation of the gospel is that we humans are more flawed and scarred than we could ever imagine, and yet more loved, cherished, and desired by God than we'll ever know. Dinah's story is one of that gospel interrupting a broken life, bringing it "up from the ashes" to kingdom fulfillment and fruitfulness. After thirty years of friendship, I confirm she is a "walking refuge" and more for many. Let her story speak deeply and stir hope for you on your journey.

—Randy Young, president and founder of The Agora Group. Cleveland, OH

Dinah Hodgson courageously invites her readers on a journey into the deeper parts of her heart, where travelers can peer into the broken windows of her soul and touch the distant echoes of brokenness in their own. *Up from the Ashes* is a call to allow the love and power of God in Christ to heal, deliver, and free us all until we are restored to our original design and purposes to the praise of His glory.

—Susan Carlton, PhDc, BCBC

You are
such a blessing
to me and all those
around you!
Much Blessings,
Dinah
Ephesians
3:20-21

Up from the
ASHES

DINAH LEE HODGSON

Up from the ASHES

RECLAIMING GOD'S
ORIGINAL DESIGN
AND PURPOSE
FOR YOUR LIFE

REDEMPTION
PRESS

ISBN 13: 978-1-64645-554-6 (Paperbook)
        978-1-64645-553-9 (ePub)
        978-1-64645-552-2 (Mobi)
        978-1-64645-538-6 (Audiobook)

LCCN: 2022909611

Dedication

To my God who has loved me from the beginning,
redeemed and rescued me, then brought me
up from the ashes and is enabling me to fulfill
the purpose and dreams He placed in my heart.
I love you and am forever grateful.

To my beloved husband, John, who has always loved,
supported, and encouraged me to follow my heart.
Thank you for always being a partner in dream
realization, my biggest cheerleader, and always loving me
so selflessly. I love you forever and always.

To my beloved children, Matt, Chris, and Catie.
I am blessed beyond measure to be your mom
and am so proud of who you are, who you are
becoming, and beyond grateful God shared you
with me. You have all made me a better person,
and you are partners in building a new, incredible legacy
for our family. I love you forever and always.

To my beloved siblings, Nominee, Tone, Doug, and Eth.
We have gone through so much together, and I'm so
thankful we were together and grateful for your love and
support throughout everything. You are amazing!
I love you forever and always.

And to all who have experienced their own ashes and
need hope. May the Lord meet you in the pages of my
story and renew your hope as He brings you
up from your ashes.

Contents

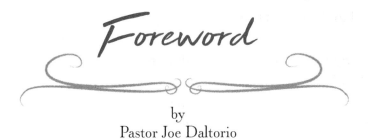

Foreword

by
Pastor Joe Daltorio

There have been many authors who have written accounts of suffering and overcoming. Some have written about spiritual and emotional healing. A few have written about their journey of being set free from spiritual strongholds and breaking generational patterns of sin, addiction, and abuse. Dinah Hodgson has written a rare book that touches on all of these.

Part memoir, part practical Bible application, and part personal revelation, Dinah has written a powerful book exploring God's design for our lives and Satan's plan to sabotage it.

Raised by the wayward daughter of New York socialite, Dinah experienced horrific childhood traumas. Without self-pity, she courageously explores the road she has traveled to great healing through the grace and power of God.

I first met Dinah at a Christian leadership conference many years ago, where I was impressed by her hunger to know God and the truth of His Word. Several years later I was so delighted when Dinah and her husband, John, walked into our church and announced they had moved back to northeast Ohio.

In February 2015, Dinah joined our pastoral staff as an associate pastor working with our Freedom Prayer Ministry and pastoral counseling. She was also tasked with the assignment of developing a prayer team equipped to help people find healing in body, soul, and spirit. The words of Jesus in Luke 4:18–19 became their mission: "The Spirit of the Lord is upon Me, because He has anointed Me to preach the gospel to the poor; He has sent Me to heal the brokenhearted, to proclaim liberty to the captives and recovery of sight to the blind, to set at liberty those who are oppressed; to proclaim the acceptable year of the Lord" (NKJV).

Over the years, I saw Dinah grow in spiritual maturity and leadership. She took advantage of every training opportunity, bringing together many resources for healing. I will never forget the night I heard her share her own journey of pain, struggle, and breaking through to freedom and healing of the heart and mind. The power of her own story has impacted so many others immobilized by shame and fear.

Dinah's ministry has touched the lives of hundreds of people in our church and in other churches and organizations where she and her team lead people to spiritual freedom and emotional healing. More importantly, she has trained many others to do the same work she has been doing.

Up from the Ashes is a strategic and powerful book for this generation. It is a message of healing, overcoming, and forgiveness the world needs to hear right now.

Read this book for leisure and interest, and you will be inspired.

Read it with a hungry, open heart, apply its principles, and you will be transformed.

Joseph M. Daltorio
Senior pastor and founder of River of Life Church in Hudson, Ohio

Acknowledgments

Writing this book was two decades in germination and never something I thought I could accomplish. There's a saying that seems appropriate for this context: "It takes a village." In my case it surely did.

Thank you to my husband, John Hodgson, who helped in so many ways and enabled me to finish the book.

Thank you to Catie Hodgson, Linda Powlison, Suzanne Dodd, Becky Young, Vicki Isaac, Stephanie Pavlantos, Janice Daltorio, and Engela Hepworth, who never wavered in their support and encouragement.

Thank you to all the prayer warriors who were instrumental in the birth of this book.

Thank you to Melanie Shaniuk for her assistance and support of the book.

Thank you to Carole Leatham for her support and connections, Athena Dean Holtz for her trust and belief in this project, Debbie Alsdorf for her expertise and holding my hand throughout the writing, Dori Harrell, Carol Tetzlaff, and the rest of the Redemption Press tribe for all they did to make this book a reality.

Thank you to Dr. Karen from Primus University who provided the opportunity and impetus to finally put what was in my heart onto paper.

Thank you to all who helped me see and grow in God's truth—

Dianna Yost, Tony Stephens, Dave Buehring, Gary Spicer, Steve Isaac, Joseph Daltorio, Randy Young, and so many others through various other means, too many to mention.

Most of all, thank you to God—Father, Son, and Holy Spirit—who saved me, cleansed me, restored me, and set my feet on a firm foundation. You gave me hope when I had none, enabled me to have a life I never could have imagined, and accomplished the unimaginable. I am forever yours, and may you receive all the glory from this redeemed life.

Introduction

The thief comes only to steal and kill and destroy.
I came that they may have life and
have it abundantly.
John 10:10

I can still hear the words of a dear woman, spoken decades ago, echoing in my heart: "You are the perfect family." Those words, meant in all sincerity as a compliment, were quite far from the truth. Little did she know that her eyes only saw what was on the surface: three adorable children dressed in their Sunday best with their nicely attired mother and father. I should know. I was the mother.

What that well-meaning woman couldn't see was the internal devastation. We did look like the perfect family. We were living the American dream. Our life consisted of a house in a lovely neighborhood, a family dog, a station wagon filled with adorable kids, a handsome husband who was a respectable physician, and a stay-at-home mom. That's the dream, right?

There was only one problem—the Easter picture. I hate that picture. I hate it because if you really look at it, you'll see the truth. I still see the picture in my mind's eye, even though I haven't looked at it in decades. I remember it all too well.

Why I never tore it up is a mystery. I guess maybe because it was a marker of sorts. Doesn't everyone take their yearly family picture, capturing the moment when they are all gussied up in our finery? We were no different. I wanted that moment frozen in time so I would be able to look back and remember my beloved children and husband as they were then. At least that is what I thought I wanted before I looked at the picture and saw the expression on my face. It was an expression of blankness, veiled anger, and lack of joy or exuberance. The expression spoke volumes. I now dub it my "Ice Queen" picture, and it definitely has become a marker. A marker of where I was and also of how far my loving heavenly Father has brought me.

This book is about how God took me from where I was in that picture and brought me "up from the ashes" and into abundant life.

I knew I was living the dream. I was showered with blessings. I had three healthy, beautiful children, a husband who faithfully loved us and provided for us, a beautiful home, and an extended network of family and friends. That was the dream I had desired all my life, so imagine my confusion and surprise as I looked at that picture and realized that although I was a blessed woman, my heart said something very different and my outside did not match my internal reality. It began to dawn on me that I was in trouble and that something was not right, although I had no concept of what that something might be.

This initiated the beginning of a journey that would encourage me to embrace the truth of the devastating and long-lasting impact of my childhood. Unlike other journeys I had prepared for, I was not bubbling over with excitement as I gathered the necessary items and outfits to pack in my matching luggage. No, this journey was one of grief, sorrow, despair, and tears as I *un*packed the baggage of a traumatic childhood. This was not a journey of my choosing.

Let's be honest—none of us choose our family of origin and its dynamics. Don't get me wrong—I love my family dearly, but what my siblings and I experienced was crazy, and it wouldn't even register on God's scale of His original intent and design for the family. The injustices we experienced would land people in jail if they happened today.

As I look back on the wrongs I experienced as a child, I am reminded of the book of Genesis and the life of Joseph, for he also suffered many injustices, and his were at the hands of his brothers and those he served.

How he must have suffered in the pit of despair through his trials and betrayals from those he loved and called family, and from spending years in servitude and imprisonment through no fault of his own!

I can only imagine the conditions he endured and the myriad of emotions that must have been like waves assailing him. I can almost hear the cry of Joseph's heart: "Why, God?" Still, through those years, Joseph continued to believe and trust God. He didn't let his heart harden because of what he experienced. How did he do this?

Maybe you have experienced injustices as Joseph did. Oh, they may not be exactly the same, but injustices they remain. How have you coped with them? Have you emerged on the other side, or are you struggling as I did and as many do? I can assure you there is hope.

As we read further into Joseph's story, we are struck by the reality that God never forgot Joseph, despite the fact that he was in prison. God was faithful to Joseph and used his experiences to form a divine character in him. At the right time, God fulfilled His plan through Joseph's life. Through circumstances orchestrated by God, Joseph was released from prison and became the second-in-command under Pharaoh.

When Joseph was later confronted by his brothers, who had abused him, he said a very interesting thing: "As for you, you meant evil against me, but God meant it for good in order to bring about this present result, to keep many people alive" (Genesis 50:20 NASB).

What in the world did he mean? Joseph had been thrown into a pit and sold into slavery by his brothers, and he was later sent to prison to languish for years for something he didn't do. How could he possibly see these injustices as being meant for good by God? How can the injustices in your life, and mine, be used for good?

It's hard to fathom how this can be, but let's backtrack for a minute. God created you, He created me, He created Joseph, and He created all of mankind. Jeremiah 29:11 tells us that He did so with "plans for [our] welfare and not for evil, to give [us] a future and a hope." God has an original design and purpose for each of us. When God designed us, He put abilities, talents, and gifts in us that would enable us to fulfill the design and possibilities He intended for our lives. I can only imagine what wonderful plans were in the heart of God when He designed me. I know that plan is for good.

Unfortunately, just as God has plans for our lives, there is an enemy of God and all of mankind who has plans and schemes to destroy our lives. We are told in John 10:10 that "the thief comes only to steal and kill and destroy." Satan's plan is to destroy mankind and separate us from God. He wants to hurt the heart of God by destroying His beloved people. From the moment we are conceived, Satan begins to personally attack each of us in order to destroy the plan and purpose of God in our lives. Just as with his plan to destroy Joseph's life, Satan has a counterplan for our lives to prevent us from fulfilling the destiny God has for us.

However, what we learn from Joseph's story is that although the Enemy had an evil plan for his life and tried to destroy it, God had other plans, and He worked not only for Joseph's good, but also for the good of his family and all of Egypt. God was faithful to Joseph and did for Joseph what He will do for us, which is "immeasurably more than all we ask or imagine, according to His power that is at work within us" (Ephesians 3:20 NIV). God restored Joseph to a position and plan that was so much more than Joseph could ever have dreamed or imagined! What God did for Joseph in the midst of injustice, He did for me, and He can also do for you.

The second half of John 10:10 tells us that Jesus "came that they may have life and have it abundantly." When I think back on my "Ice Queen" picture, I know that my face clearly revealed that I did not have the abundant life God promises. My heart was shut down, despite all the blessings, by the injustices and schemes the Enemy had mined in my life to keep me from the abundant life and destiny God designed.

More than two decades ago, I had a chance encounter. It was the seed that would germinate into this book. I was at a ministry gathering and was chatting with another woman. As we talked, a third woman, whom I casually knew, walked by. She stopped, turned around, came back, and stood in front of me. Looking intently into my eyes, she asked, "Have you ever considered writing?"

I laughed and quickly quipped back, "If you knew more about me, you wouldn't ask!" What she didn't know was that as a child, I had struggled with a learning disability in English (although I had only realized it as an adult). It continued to be a source of self-consciousness.

Not knowing my thoughts, she simply replied, "God wanted me to ask you," and then she walked off.

That question haunted me. God, in His goodness (despite my angst and insecurity about writing), miraculously cleared the way to fulfill a piece of the plan He has for my life. God did immeasurably more than I could ever hope or imagine. He took my life, a life bruised and battered by people unknowingly being used in the schemes of the Enemy, and redeemed it for good—not just for my good, but also for the good of others. I learned firsthand that no one is beyond God's love, faithfulness, and restoration.

My hope is that just as God has brought me to a place of healing, restored destiny, and abundant life, so, too, you might discover that God wants the same for you. If my life story can be of any benefit to you, then I will count it an honor and a privilege to have walked with you.

Part 1

Lost and Found

The Miraculous
Here and Now

*Now to him who is able to do far more abundantly
than all that we ask or think, according to the power
at work within us, to him be glory in the church
and in Christ Jesus throughout all generations,
forever and ever. Amen.*
Ephesians 3:20-21

I shouldn't be in this place. No, I'm serious. I should not be living the life that I am. I have defied the odds, and I am living an incredibly abundant and fulfilled life.

It is not that my life has been perfect by any stretch of the imagination. On the contrary, it has been broken. It has been filled with despair, isolation, divorce, and poverty of heart and soul, with a lot of broken relationships left in its wake.

I am a living testament that what you are told is not always what you should believe. The circumstances of my life—or should I say, of my childhood—could very well have put me on a very different trajectory.

I grew up in a dysfunctional family that included physical, emotional, and sexual abuse. Although there was definitely a semblance of love and privilege, there was also an overwhelming amount of chaos, confusion, instability, anger, rejection, and abuse. I'm grateful for all that was good and

> **Every experience in life has the potential to either break you or be used as a deep reservoir for the benefit of yourself and others.**

beneficial, but thankfully, I can also look back and be grateful for the pain and suffering. It is not that I'm glad it all happened, but because of it, I am who I am today. I have learned that every experience in life has the potential to either break you or to be used as a deep reservoir for your own benefit and the benefit of others.

The truth and predictions made by professionals do not account for the fact that there is an alternative truth—a truth that is greater and more powerful and crushes human-based predictions, revealing them for what they are: well-intentioned, but erroneous, attempts at truth.

My life makes folly of man's predictions, and it unearths the reality that there is a God who is real, who loves people, and who has a purpose, plan, and destiny filled with hope for every individual on the planet. Over and over again in my life, God's truth has proven to be real, powerful, personal, and transformative.

While I was in college, my life was earmarked for destruction, and I was confronted by God. Putting myself in God's hands and believing what He says has worked miracles in my life. Although I suffered much as a child, His transformative power restored my broken heart and gave me a life that is filled with hope, fulfillment, and abundance.

If you are anything like me, you want to get from point A to point B in the quickest way possible. It was no different for me during this process of restoration and abundance. I wanted to go from suffering and brokenness to destiny and fruit-filled living as quickly as possible. Unfortunately, this journey is not typically instantaneous or easy. It feels more like a roller coaster with highs and lows, free falls, and twisty turns. Sometimes you wish you could change your mind and get off the ride.

I am so thankful that I was not alone on this journey. God never left me. Many times He carried me through when I was too tired and no longer had strength to go on. When I see people get off a physical roller coaster, they are often laughing and filled with exuberance. Even though my ride with the Lord isn't over, I feel much the same way as I look back over the years. I have deep gratitude for God, who has faithfully and lovingly brought me through depths of pain and has placed me in a rich life.

How do I know? Have you ever seen before-and-after pictures in magazines? Looking at my life is like looking at those pictures. I can attest to the fact that I am not the same person I used to be. I have regained my voice. I have a marriage of forty-two years, I have the legacy of spectacular children and grandchildren, and I am walking in fruitful ministry. This was not where I was originally headed. I was once a broken, struggling woman, but God graciously and miraculously transformed me into who I am today.

> **Graciously, God transformed me from a broken, struggling woman to the miraculous here and now.**

Finding My Voice

You may be asking, "What did He do?" or "How did He do it?" I would love to shout the answers from the mountaintop for all to hear! That in and of itself *is* the miracle.

As a toddler, my voice was stolen from me. I don't mean literally. I could still speak, but I was placed in so much fear that I was too afraid to give voice to who I was, what I thought, or what was going on. I'm not talking about superficial things, but about my deep inner life and circumstances.

If my mom were alive today, she would probably tell you that my voice was anything but stolen. However, she didn't know. She didn't see, and she most certainly didn't understand at the time.

I was told by my abuser that I would be killed if I ever spoke about anything that happened or that the cops would come and take me to jail and I would never see my family again. If you know the trusting heart of a child, you understand why these words did not seem like idle threats. They were truth to my little heart, and they served their purpose to shut me up.

Even as a young adult, I would shake as I spoke truth. I was so afraid of saying anything that revealed myself or reality. Growing up, if

I was in a crowd, I was much more comfortable fading into the woodwork. I would shrink back, hoping no one would notice me. I became the lost child who had no voice. Silence was my safety.

It has been a long road to finding my voice—a true miracle that God has worked in my heart. Despite the fears and downright terror that I felt throughout the years, God has now brought me up to center stage, sometimes even speaking in front of hundreds of people. Where I once was speechless and bound with fear, not willing to step up to the plate, God has lovingly nurtured me and has shown me that He is with me and that I will not be destroyed, killed, or separated from my family for telling the truth.

I remember one of the first times I spoke in front of several hundred people. Obviously, I lived to tell the tale. My husband and I were leading a mission team to Swaziland, now known as the Kingdom of Eswatini. We went to renovate a small house for orphans and hold a leadership conference for community leaders. Back then, speaking in front of people caused me much anxiety and required hours of preparation. Every word had to be written out verbatim to quell my angst, but the manual labor on the orphan house left little time for conference preparation.

Stepping up onto the stage that morning with the bare bones of an outline clutched in my hand, I clung to a trust that God could speak through me.

As the day of the conference dawned, I was a bundle of nerves. Stepping up onto the stage that morning with the bare bones of an outline clutched in my hand, I clung to a trust that God could speak through me. I don't even remember what I said that day, but I do remember having a tangible sense that God's smile and love radiated over me as I spoke. Many people told me how anointed my message was. Personally, I felt I had a destiny moment—a moment when I felt that I was doing something I was designed for.

That experience didn't cure me, but it gave me a taste of God's design for my life. I am so thankful that God helped me get up on the stage that day and that He proved Himself faithful.

Years later, I can say that God has completely restored my voice and has freed me to speak His truth without fear. I have spoken nationally and internationally, sometimes in front of a few people and sometimes in front of hundreds. I have taught and preached, and although I often still feel butterflies in the pit of my stomach, I have surprisingly discovered that I love speaking and sharing God's truth.

What is even more telling is that the people I find it difficult to speak to and share my heart with are also now recipients of my message. Although an enemy disguised in my abuser's body tried to steal my voice and the purpose God had for it, I am determined to no longer be held back and silenced.

Have you ever felt that your voice was stolen? I know how challenging this is, but I also know that your voice doesn't have to be stolen forever—because God is ready and willing to help you find it again.

Acquiring Healthy Relational Reference Points

Being raised by parents who were never married and who had a track record of broken relationships left me with no reference point for a healthy marriage. As a child, I experienced hatred, conflict, crashing boundaries, and oversexualization—with some fun and love thrown in. Considering this background, it is no surprise that I was set up for failure in relationships. This proved to be true—until God intervened.

Soon after God entered my life during my senior year of nursing school, I met the man who would become my husband. It was truly a miracle that I met him, but even more so, it was a miracle that we married and have been married for forty-two years so far. Only God could do this.

I was so broken that I was incredibly afraid of men, even though I longed to be in a relationship and get married. My usual pattern would be to date a guy (although I have not dated many, I can assure you), and within months break it off because subconsciously I was terrified. It was a real push-me, pull-you experience—until God got involved and brought John, a senior medical student, into my life.

Our first meeting was miraculously orchestrated by God. From the start, it was different with John. Almost immediately, I knew I would marry him. I didn't realize it at the time, but God had perfectly matched us and intersected our lives at just the right moment.

However, the miracle of our meeting is not where the miracle ended. I have already given you a hint about my childhood, but sadly, John also had a somewhat dysfunctional background. When John was a young boy, his father died, and John's growing-up years were marked with a less-than-desirable stepfather and emotional trauma. Thankfully, though, he had a devoted mother.

Aside from those very real challenges, John, as a medical student, had many years of intensive, time-consuming training and practice ahead of him. The sobering statistic of a 50 percent divorce rate for medical marriages added an additional strike against our marriage. Humanly speaking, our marriage was heavily weighted toward failure.

However, when John and I said our vows "until death do us part" at the altar, we meant them. God, in partnership with us, enabled us to face our baggage by coming together instead of clashing and breaking apart.

Sometimes it was only our deep commitment and love for each other and God that pushed us through the obstacles that boldly battered our marriage.

It hasn't always been easy. Sometimes it was only our deep commitment and love for each other and for God that pushed us through the obstacles that boldly battered our marriage. Looking at our lives today, we realize that our love has grown deeper and our marriage has prospered. We have shared a wealth of memories and have amazing children and grandchildren. I can truly say that my life is rich because of God's relational restoration. All those dreams I had as a child for a normal, healthy family (whatever normal is) are now being realized.

I am amazed at the miracle God worked. He took a little girl from a broken home, who had few healthy relational tools, and He placed her in a relationship that resulted in a thriving family. It truly is incredible, and God can surely do for you what He did for me.

How do I know? There is a Bible verse that I have held on to over the years: "For God shows no partiality" (Romans 2:11). God doesn't show favoritism, so what He did for someone else, He did for me; and what He did for me, I am completely confident He will do for you

Shifting My Heritage to a Lasting Legacy

I recently heard a wise, godly woman by the name of Marion In-gegneri explain the difference between heritage and legacy. She said that heritage refers to the life you were born into—the "cards you were dealt" as a child. In contrast, legacy is what you do with your heritage and the type of impact your life makes.[1]

If you are like me, you may have a dream of leaving a lasting impact on the world. I used to think that this impact only had to do with what we did through our careers and vocations. I've come to realize, though, that most of the influence I will make is through my children and grandchildren. Growing up, I loved playing with dolls as well as playing house. My pretend family always had a wonderful husband and lots of children. This playing was closely tied to my ever-constant dream of becoming a wife and mother. Somehow, I never doubted that this would be part of my life.

Despite never talking about this with John before we got married, I was certainly glad to learn after we were married that John wanted children as much as I did. After four years of marriage, I became pregnant. Over the years, our family burgeoned to include two amazing sons, Matthew and Christopher, and a wonderful daughter, Caitlin. They are and always will be treasures of my heart! I don't have to tell any parent, whether spiritual, foster, adoptive, or biological, that parenting is not for the faint of heart. Like most parents, I had dreams and hopes for my kids, and I especially never wanted them to experience the type of pain that I had experienced as a child.

> Like most parents, I had dreams and hopes for my kids, and I especially never wanted them to experience the type of pain that I had as a child.

Unfortunately, I entered parenting with only minimal tools in my parenting toolbox. When all you have is a hammer, possibly a screwdriver, and no instructions, it's hard to raise healthy, happy children. Although I tried very hard and, thankfully, did many things right as a mom, I am also well aware that I fumbled my way through.

I passionately wanted to be the perfect mother and to give my kids a heritage that was better than mine. However, my repressed wounds and pain splashed all over them. The saying "wounded people wound others" is indeed true, and it was an unintentional reality of my mothering. I was certainly not the perfect mother I had dreamed I would be or wanted to be.

Knowing the challenges my kids had to navigate through because of my dysfunction and wounded heart, I am humbled and forever grateful that I am called their mom. My heart sings along with Maria von Trapp in *The Sound of Music*: "I must have done something good." Now seeing our children as adults fills me with awe. They have truly become amazing individuals, and I am deeply proud of them. Each one is uniquely engaged in following their dreams, and they are not just outstanding in what they do, but they are also really remarkable people. With tears in my eyes, I can say that God was faithful to fill in the scattered holes left by my parenting and that my children have become extraordinary individuals.

Aside from being one of the best gifts of my life, my children have showered me with many treasured blessings throughout their lives. None are as special as the grandchildren they have given John and me, along with the privilege of being able to watch them as parents. Observing them with their children fills me with a sense of wonder because they are ten times better at parenting than I ever was. As I observe them, I marvel that God faithfully took the ashes of my life and created a beautiful legacy in my children and grandchildren.

Take heart, because God *will* be faithful as you call out to Him and invite Him to do what only He can do, the miraculous.

Most parents want the absolute best for their children and grandchildren. Much like I did, you might find yourself struggling with parenthood because of your background. Take heart, for God will be faithful as you call out to Him and invite Him to do what only He can do—the miraculous.

Discovering My Purpose

On the topic of the miraculous, a new (and I'm talking "we just met" new) young friend recently gave me an amazing compliment as a small group of us enjoyed a meal and shared affirmations around the table. He said, "You are a walking refuge." He proceeded to relay his impression that I not only see people as they are currently, but I also see their potential in God.

I was taken aback. With tears in his eyes, a longtime friend proclaimed, "He nailed you." I was amazed that someone I had talked to for only a few hours had paid me such a tribute. I can't think of many words of praise that would mean as much to me since God refers to Himself as a "refuge" in Psalm 62:8.

Merriam-Webster defines "refuge" as "a shelter or protection from danger or distress; a place that provides shelter or protection."[2] How could someone so broken now be called a "walking refuge," a place of shelter or protection?

For decades, I have prayed that people would see God in me, and here I was faced with the realization that God *was* continuing to work the miraculous in me by answering that prayer. However, "looking like" and representing God was not always the dream I aspired to.

> However, "looking like" and representing God was not always the dream I aspired to.

As children, we all have ideas about what we want to be when we grow up. A fireman, doctor, nurse, mommy, dancer, construction worker, or princess is what often rolls off little tongues. I was no different. I was determined to be a nurse. It's a bit embarrassing to think of how this dream transpired because it shows my immature ability to sense God's leading. On the other hand, it reveals determination and a desire to help others.

When I was a little girl, my family had a much-loved caregiver named Sarah. We siblings often remember her for her fried chicken and sweetened iced tea. I definitely remember that with fondness (and activated salivary glands), but her impact of love was much greater. God also indirectly used her to speak destiny into my life.

Sarah would watch soap operas while fulfilling her tasks. As a six-year-old, I watched Nurse Jessie Brewer on *General Hospital* care for patients and help them feel better. In my young mind, I interpreted the drama unfolding before my little eyes as a nurse taking people's pain away.

At this ripe young age, I decided that I would become a nurse and wipe out people's pain so they wouldn't suffer like I did. Throughout the subsequent years, I never wavered from this childhood decision. With my heart set, no one saw the need to counsel me with different possibilities.

I will never regret my decision to become a nurse because I learned lifelong skills—and I met my beloved husband—during my training.

As a child, I think I sensed God's calling to minister to others, but I immaturely put it in the only box I knew—nursing. Years later, after many hours of studying the Bible and volunteering in various church positions, I realized that God's call on my heart was ministry, specifically helping individuals grow in the understanding of God and His character, ways, and mission. This realization came when I was taking a course called "Women with a Call" at a local Bible training center.

It is such an amazing experience to have God open your eyes to glimmers of your destiny and how He uniquely crafted you for it.

Taking the course ostensibly to answer questions our church had about specific roles for women in the church, I never anticipated that God would use it to point me toward a life purpose. I had a true "aha" moment and a new understanding about why I am the way I am. It is such an amazing experience to have God open your eyes to glimmers of your destiny and how He uniquely crafted you for it.

With this new insight, I started badgering God with the question, *What is my ministry?* One thing I've learned is that if we ask God a question, He will surely answer it. It might not necessarily be in the way we imagine, but He will definitely answer.

I'll never forget His quiet response: "You are your ministry."

What did that mean? I was not sure, so me being me, I kept asking:

What is my ministry?

Persistence is a good thing, right? His response was always the same. Was I just being ignorant, or might I not have gotten God's point? Either way, I was at a loss.

As I think back, I can't help but laugh. Have you ever had one of those times when someone keeps bugging you for an answer, and you finally blurt one out in exasperation? That's what I think God did with me. It was not so much in exasperation as tongue in cheek, with a twinkle in His eye.

This is what He said: "Isaiah 61."

Isaiah 61? What? With Bible in hand, I turned to Isaiah 61. These words jumped off the page at me:

> The Spirit of the Lord God is upon me, because the Lord has anointed me to bring good news to the poor; he has sent me to bind up the brokenhearted, to proclaim liberty to the captives, and the opening of the prison to those who are bound; to proclaim the year of the Lord's favor, and the day of vengeance of our God; to comfort all who mourn; to grant to those who mourn in Zion—to give them a beautiful headdress instead of ashes, the oil of gladness instead of mourning, the garment of praise instead of a faint spirit; that they may be called oaks of righteousness, the planting of the Lord, that he may be glorified. They shall build up the ancient ruins; they shall raise up the former devastations; they shall repair the ruined cities, the devastations of many generations. (Isaiah 61:1–4)

As I read the passage over and over, it seemed substantive. It was something I could sink my teeth into. Yet in all honesty, I had no idea what God was telling me.

Quite frankly, I pride myself on being fairly quick to figure things out. Obviously, though, I did not do so in this case. It took me more than a year to discover that this passage pointed to the life of Christ and was fulfilled in Luke 4.

When I queried the Lord, He impressed upon me that His call on my life was twofold. First, He highlighted that as a Christian, I was to represent Christ to the world. Secondly, I was to walk in the ways of Christ and do the things He did. He was speaking to me of both essence (being) and function (doing).

The concept of my "being the ministry" related to both essence and function. Essentially, I was to *do* the work of the ministry—His mission—which had everything to do with Isaiah 61. I was also to *be* like Christ—His character and His ways of being—to those around me. That seemed to be a tall order! However, I knew that if God called me to do it, as impossible as it seemed, He would enable me as well.

Walking through the decades since, I have clung to two promises: "With God all things are possible" (Matthew 19:26), and "He who began a good work in you will bring it to completion at the day of Jesus Christ" (Philippians 1:6). These promises buoyed me over the years when the waves of doubt and discouragement washed over me when I saw little progress in Christ being formed in me or felt frustration at not seeing fruit from pouring myself out in the work of the ministry.

Fast forward to my new friend's comment: "You are a walking refuge." I felt sideswiped by his observation, for it caused me to face the fact that God was actually working His character in me. I quickly recalled the opportunities I'd had to minister and live out Isaiah 61 to many people during the previous decades. There were women who had been trafficked in Benin, Africa, who needed to learn how to gain freedom in Christ and how to reenter society with a marketable trade. I had the privilege of ministering to them as well as proclaiming the good news to many others. I have had the opportunity to minister to orphans in South Africa, to meet weekly with doctors' wives in Cleveland, to teach Freedom Prayer classes to church members, and to be a part of many personal prayer sessions with people seeking help at the altar or in private.

I actually *was* binding up and comforting the brokenhearted and helping to bring individuals to new levels of freedom. Despite my life having been doomed to destruction, I saw clear evidence that God *had* done great things in and through me.

My heart is filled with thanksgiving as I reflect on where my life was, what God has done, and how He uses me as an instrument of His love and care to those around me. My life is truly a miracle. God's love in and through me is undeserved, yet is freely given.

My here and now is to be celebrated, but I echo the apostle Paul's words:

> Not that I have already obtained this or am already perfect, but I press on to make it my own, because Christ Jesus has made me His own. Brothers [and sisters], I do not consider that I have made it my own. But one thing I do: forgetting what lies behind and straining forward to what lies ahead, I press on toward the goal for the prize of the upward call of God in Christ Jesus. (Philippians 3:12–14)

What do you think of your here and now? Are you celebrating the miraculous things God has done or is doing in your life? Or are you struggling with issues that are overwhelming to you and of which you see no end in sight? Or maybe you, like me, are celebrating and pressing on toward the goal while fully cognizant that life will be filled with its ups and downs.

Wherever you find yourself, I wish I could sit down and chat with you over a cup of tea or coffee and hear your story. Those who know me would confirm that this is what I love to do!

I know One who loves you deeply while knowing everything about you, and He is able to do immeasurably more than you could hope, dream, or imagine. He is ready anywhere and anytime to sit with you, listen to your heart, surround you with His love, give you the encouragement you may be thirsting for, and make your here and now miraculous.

I know One who loves you deeply while knowing everything about you, and He is able to do immeasurably more than you could hope, dream, or imagine.

Now that I've given an overview of my journey, let's dig deeper into how things got off track as well as look at the process God used to bring me into His destiny.

Destiny Lost

After you have suffered a little while, the God of all grace,
who has called you to his eternal glory in Christ,
will himself restore, confirm, strengthen, and establish you.
1 Peter 5:10

Before we can experience a miraculous here and now and be the image bearers God has designed us to be, we must explore the dynamics of our background and its influence in shaping who we have become. If we want to grow, I honestly believe that this exploration will never end. We will continually need to shed the garments of our past that stand in the way of our moving forward.

This journey is not one I relish. It is often painful. Have you heard the saying, "No pain, no gain"? I don't know about you, but I have found much truth in it. To move forward, it is sometimes necessary to look at our past. So here we go!

So alone. Alone, crouching in the corner on a dark, cold, cement basement floor. All alone in a world where no one sees. The world rushes by and doesn't bother . . . not even glancing and spotting this poor little girl so tender—left defenseless in a cold, dark world. Who notices the burden she carries like an overstuffed backpack on a small, fragile body? No one is troubled by the pain that grips her like a bony hand with thin, gnarly fingers and won't let go. She is stuck; alone in that corner, discarded, usefulness lost, and hated for what she is. Confusion swarms her along with a deep longing for someone to perceive the depths of sadness, despair, and grief that pool and overflow her heart like a dam about to burst. Lost and alone. Searching. Is there one who will take note of this little one trapped and stuck, and reach out a hand of comfort and arms of shelter? Is there not one who can bring light to her darkness, beauty to her ugliness, and hope to her despair? She looks and longs, and sees not one.

(Excerpt from my journal entry)

Chaos Reigns

From the very beginning, my life was filled with chaos, and I felt much like the little girl represented in my journal. It would take hours to give a full picture; even I don't see it all, so I'll touch on a few critical highlights:

- My mom was a victim of childhood neglect and abuse, sustaining wounds and scars that exploded on those she was closest to—her children!

- My mother married Marvin Stephens and had two children: Melanie and Anthony, my older siblings. Marvin and Mom were part of a theater company—a wild and crazy (my words) group of people who, from my perspective, practiced "free love." For some, it was apparently due to the therapy they received from a Reichian therapist.

- My brother Doug and I were illegitimate—the product of "therapy" and an adulterous affair my mother had with our father, Richard Keeler, who was also a member of the theater company.

- Divorcing Marvin in the mid-1950s, my mom became a twenty-eight-year-old single mom with four children under the age of four-and-a-half. That was definitely not acceptable back then!

- My father, Richard, was raised in a dysfunctional family. As a young man, he was a gunner in a B-29 bomber during the Korean War. Seemingly, his way of drowning his emotional pain was to turn to theater, work, sex, girlfriends, and pornography.

- When I was five years old, my father officially adopted Doug and me, changing our last name from Stephens to Keeler. With one stroke of the judge's pen, our identity and lives changed forever.

- When I was nine, my mother married our school shop teacher, Bernie, and had my little brother, Ethan. Shortly thereafter, they moved the family away from the Philadelphia area and our fathers to Martha's Vineyard.

These represent just some of the significant components of my life story. Conveying my history in bullet points is purposeful. I want to accentuate that as a child and into my adult years, I could rattle off personal history as one would unemotionally recite memorized historical data. Many young, wounded children, like I was, learn to repress their emotions and reduce their lives to a list of facts. This is not what God intends or desires for us! My mother, an only child, was raised in a prominent affluent family of New York City society. She had to behave just right. Children spoke only when spoken to, and they did as they were told.

As a proper daughter, Mom attended the right schools, wore the right clothes, and did the right things. However, once married—much to my grandmother's dismay—Mom threw off her upbringing, rebelled against her background, pursued her passion for theater, and subsequently joined a small theatre company.

Theater was my mother and father's passion. There is no denying that they were gifted artists. Many people have been the recipients of their talent. For me, theater was truly a mixed bag.

But wait! I'm getting ahead of myself. Let's get back to history. I definitely have good childhood memories of the theatre life. Nevertheless, when I call theater people "the crazies," it is based on living through the aftermath of their crazy actions. I don't lay the responsibility for their folly solely at their feet, as I'm not sure they would have delved so fully into aberrant behavior if such behavior had not been encouraged by the Reichian therapist they counseled with.

I have no doubt that the recommended "therapy" was considered to be therapeutic by the therapist, but I have a different term for it: abuse. The therapist's focus was on helping his clients pull out the sexual energy they were suppressing, rendering them healthier emotionally. However, it gave them the freedom to do whatever felt good to them and break free from binding inhibitions. In my mind, it was free license for guiltless sex and adulterous relationships.

My brother Doug and I were the consequence of such therapy; we were two "oops" from a prolonged affair with my father, Richard. I can't say that I'm sorry we were born, but the repercussions of this behavior were monumental. There was the breakup of a marriage, mass chaos, devastation, alcoholism, overt sexual behavior, and emotional damage not only to my siblings and me, but I'm sure to many others who were directly and indirectly involved.

These beginnings alone would have been traumatic enough. However, chaos swarmed around my mother's life with her explosive rages, volatility, and dysfunction.

She continued seeing this "therapist" and felt that we children needed to experience this privilege, or rather, horror, as well. I know Mom meant well and had our welfare in mind, but it was anything but therapeutic. For us, what ensued during these treatments was added trauma. Imagine being taken into a room alone with this larger-than-life therapist who proceeded to have us strip to our underwear and then bound us in sheets. The goal? An emotional response! He was looking for an expression of anger, crying, something—anything so we wouldn't stuff our emotions.

Once accomplished, our therapy was considered therapeutic and the session was over. Additionally, the therapist taught my mom the technique of using "slap therapy" (my term) at home: slapping me until an emotional reaction was elicited. To this day, I remember the technique with revulsion. Therapeutic? No! Again, the word "abuse" thunders in my head. How in the world could anyone—a therapist or anyone else—believe this was healing and beneficial?

Despite the dysfunction, life in the early years seemed to be fairly cohesive, with both fathers actively engaged in our lives. We were also blessed to attend a private elementary school, where we were encircled like a loving family. Sadly, this was dramatically altered when I turned five years old.

In an act of honesty, my mom allowed my biological father to adopt Doug and me because when we were born, she was married and we had her last name, Stephens. Going before the judge, I remember answering "Yes" when asked if I wanted Dad to adopt me. What did I know? How did I know at five years old what it would mean to go from being a Stephens to a Keeler—forever then bearing the title *illegitimate*? How could I know I would carry this painful label around like a ball and chain permanently attached to my leg, never to escape from it? How could I know that this action would underscore and further separate our family into segments?

It might be difficult for many in today's progressive age to understand how traumatic those family dynamics were. Just remember that in the 1950s, it was not acceptable to be illegitimate, let alone born from an adulterous affair.

The years that followed witnessed a disorienting family life of separation and togetherness. On weekends, Doug and I stayed with our biological father, returning on Sunday to spend weekdays with Mom and our siblings. As my mother and father's relationship deteriorated to screaming and physical fights, the separation became even more distinct as bitter hatred developed between them. The segregation of our family was devastatingly painful, but so was much of the time we spent with Dad.

I loved my dad. He had many inspiring qualities. He was good-hearted, a champion of the downtrodden, creative, artistic, intelligent, and mindful of social justice. He was loving, he was an incredible storyteller, and he was an all-around dynamic personality. Many children would love a dad like this. I agree. However, as I intimated earlier, Dad wrestled with his own demons.

In the 1950s, my dad never fit the mold of my friends' fathers. He was not depicted in television shows such as *Father Knows Best* or *Leave it to Beaver*. No. Dad was not one to conform or fit any mold. He felt more comfortable in old, tattered, holey clothes sporting a ponytail and a big beer belly. Sexuality oozed from every pore of his body, along with the overwhelming and unforgettable stench of alcohol. Subsequently, the uninvited emotional guests of shame and embarrassment plagued me and our relationship.

Regrettably, Dad's good traits were overshadowed by his dysfunctional ones, which included alcoholism, workaholism, and an overt addiction to sex and pornography. In addition to these things, his girlfriends, young and old, were paraded in and out of our young lives. One of these things alone was enough to skew my emotional development. Jumbled together, they created a distorted lens through which to view relationships, identity, male and female roles, and personal worth, leaving me scarred emotionally and sexually.

Throughout these crazy, mixed-up years, my maternal grandmother became a source of stability and cohesiveness. Having gotten over my mother's choices, she fully embraced and supported not only her, but all of us. Actually, she never embraced my father.

My grandmother's support came in many forms, such as desperately needed finances, gifts, and college tuition—but more importantly, a devotion to each of us and a home on Nantucket Island. That home became a safe haven for me and a place that embodied glimmers of normality. I loved my grandmother deeply, and I am grateful for her love, care, and influence in my life.

Her home—our home—on Nantucket became a summer oasis in the sandstorm of life. It was there that I had the happiest times of my childhood and young adulthood. The days were filled with a plethora of friends, bike riding, family togetherness, swimming, tennis, and just being a kid surrounded by love in a beautiful home.

When my mom married Bernie, life was uprooted once again. Our family of seven packed up and moved to a campground and later built a cabin on Martha's Vineyard. I disliked the previous family trips we took there. Camping in the woods with outhouses and no running water was not high on my list, and it in no way compared to Nantucket and my grandmother's home. Therefore, I wasn't a fan of this new adventure.

In addition, the move meant leaving my dad. Although our relationship was convoluted, I found this separation excruciating. I went from seeing Dad every weekend to once a year. Years later, I realize that this move proved beneficial to me by reducing emotional trauma and chaos—but more on that later.

My middle and high school years seemed quasi-normal. These years can be challenging for many, and they certainly were for me. They were a mixture of loneliness and school activity. My older siblings attended a boarding school, and I had a workaholic stepfather and a mother who, having given up her beloved theater when we were young, now re-immersed herself full bore into the local theater company.

The reality was that I was alone a lot. The loneliness was real, and I often felt like a teenage orphan. In response, I threw myself into the activities of high school, and they brought great solace and joy. These activities included the tennis team, choral groups, the yearbook staff, the student council, musicals, plays, and of course, friendships. I cherished each of these activities and friendships, as well as the family times I did have. Each in their own way helped keep emotional pain and loneliness at bay.

For years, I didn't understand the emotional and spiritual impact that the details of our family background can have on our lives. I do now, though—both the good and the bad. I am thrilled for those who have experienced more good influences and am empathetic to those who experienced bad—often far worse than mine. These childhood histories become the foundations of our lives.

Crumbled Foundations

No one wants a building with a faulty foundation. It may look nice on the outside, but over time it starts to crumble. The analogy to human development proves true. Dysfunctional and chaotic childhoods may produce healthy looking children, but over time these same individuals will show unhealthy signs of their crumbled foundation.

> **The foundation laid for my life had cracks, fissures, and missing pieces, leaving me emotionally and spiritually faulty.**

This was definitely true for me. The foundation that was laid for my life had cracks, fissures, and missing pieces, leaving me emotionally and spiritually faulty. Thinking of this reminds me of the story of the three little pigs. This story scared me when I was little. However, it provides a great illustration of the importance of building houses correctly.

Later, as I read the Bible, this lesson was emphasized to me. Jesus, speaking to a crowd, exhorted the people to listen. He contended that those who listen to His words are wise and are like those who build their houses on rock. Those who don't listen are foolish and are like those who build their houses on sand. When the storms and wind come, the houses on the rock stand firm, but those on the sand fall (Matthew 7:24–27).

The engineers at Martin Perry Associates agree. They write: "Foundations are the first part of any construction. They are incredibly important to the durability of a building, and if not completed correctly, they can affect the strength and resilience of the building once completed. In short, without a stable foundation, a building will not be reliable nor last a long time."[3] So it seems that you can't get away from it: foundations, whether for a building or a life, are critically important and have long-lasting impact.

Taking a quick look through the data of my life, I see that my foundations were anything but firm and secure. I had no idea what strong life foundations looked like. As I was thinking, something from the recesses of my mind started to bubble up—something from years before. I was thinking of Maslow's hierarchy of needs.[4] Aha! Maybe this could prove useful. I hadn't heard of this until we studied it in nurse's training.

Essentially, Maslow had a theory about basic human needs and the necessity for their fulfillment. These met needs would build sequentially upon each other and would enable proper development of a healthy, functioning adult. Beginning in infancy and progressing to adulthood, these needs were:

1. *Physiological needs*: food, water, warmth, rest

2. *Safety needs*: security, safety

3. *Love and belonging*: friendship, intimacy, family, sense of connection

4. *Esteem*: respect, self-esteem, status, recognition, strength, freedom

5. *Self-actualization*: desire to become the most that one can be

Maslow's concept of these needs as critical building blocks laid down as a foundation in individuals made sense to me. His information appeared helpful in highlighting elements necessary for healthy human development.

Placing my background next to his list, I realized that my emotional development had gaping holes. As I pondered this list, I realized that something seemed to be absent in Maslow's formational foundations: the spiritual aspect of development. As a Christian, I knew that this missing piece was critical.

For years, I have been taught that humans are created in God's image (Genesis 1:26), mirroring the triune God (Father, Son, and Holy Spirit) as triune beings (body, soul, and spirit—1 Thessalonians 5:23). Therefore, I knew that the spiritual dynamic was important. Studying God's viewpoint on development would reveal a better picture of a healthy foundation formation. What better place to look than Genesis, where God's original design and intent for mankind is found?

In his book *Living Free,* Mike Riches succinctly summarizes what I discovered:

> God's original design is that we would live eternally with Him in perfect unity and fellowship, with no sorrow, no pain, no hurt, and no sickness. He planned for us to live without relational tension, heartache, sorrow, or emptiness. Instead, we were created to be fulfilled, complete, joy-filled, and at peace. God created mankind to dwell with Him.[5]

How does this happen? Human beings were designed to grow on a foundation of love and truth.[6] God's love and truth, poured out through parents and others in the lives of children, creates firm and sturdy foundations.

God's love and truth, poured out through parents and others in the lives of children, creates firm and sturdy foundations.

Absorbing all of this information was emotionally difficult. Sometimes I found it nearly impossible to allow the reality of my dysfunctional background to seep in.

Being someone who likes to organize, I began making a two-columned mental checklist of all the information I gathered. The two headings of my list were *Acquired/Experienced* and *Deficient.* This helped me identify the formational building blocks in place, or lacking, in my foundation.

Sadly, the list revealed that the blocks under the *Deficient* column far outnumbered those in the *Acquired/Experienced* column. The evidence was clearly undeniable: my foundation for life was inadequate for building a healthy adult life filled with purpose and strength.

Faulty Foundations: Creating Entrenched Thought Patterns

When personal foundations—our plumb lines of love and truth—are faulty, it is pretty clear that anything built on top of them will be askew. As children, we don't realize that our foundations are being built. We just take in experiences and absorb life as it comes.

Elaine Hunter, an early childhood development writer, explains it like this: "Children, especially in the early years, are like little sponges, absorbing all the information around them and then actively making sense of it."[7]

> **As kids, I guess we do the best we can, processing life and circumstances through our own immature lens and then formulating conclusions.**

Making sense of it! That's not only laughable, but it is challenging. How can one make sense of things when chaos reigns and there is no sense? As kids, I guess we do the best we can, processing life and circumstances through our own immature lens and then formulating conclusions. Without mature guidance, though, these conclusions are often erroneous.

Using my life as an example, I formed a plethora of subconscious assumptions about myself and life, entrenching each assumption deep into my psyche. At the time, I didn't know I was doing so. After years of excavating as an adult, I uncovered the truth that many of these unhealthy thought patterns have nothing to do with love or truth. Is this hard to grasp? It was for me. I had no clue as an adult that there was a cause-and-effect relationship between my childhood and the life I was experiencing as an adult. A snapshot of my examples might illuminate this concept.

Foundational Reality	Thought Pattern
Illegitimate birth	• I'm different, and I'm not a full-fledged member of the family or society. • I don't belong. • I perform to be accepted, but it's as if I'm never good enough.
Sexual abuse	• Dissociate to get away from pain. • I'm powerless. • I am an object and have no worth. • Tell anyone the truth, or don't do what you are told to do, and you will be killed or taken from your family. • All men want is sex. • Men are scary. • I can't say "No." • Perform correctly—even if you don't know how.
Multi-father family with single mom	• I'm different. • I'm unacceptable.
Unavailable parents/workaholism/ limited parental involvement (especially as a teen)	• I'm not worth attention. • I'm invisible. • I'm not lovable. • I am on my own.
Parents' physical fights/mother's rages	• Anger is terrifying, avoid at all costs. • Keep the peace.

Even now as I compose this list, despite all that God has done in my life, residual sadness hits me like a ton of bricks. To go through life with so many negative and unhealthy thought patterns felt like growing up with my hands and feet tied while being thrown into deep water. I was fighting with all my strength to stay afloat.

Do you remember the little girl at the beginning of the chapter? I felt like her for much of my life. I felt alone, abandoned, and unable to escape the deeply embedded destructive messages that filled my mind because of poorly formed childhood foundations.

Faulty Foundations: Life and Destiny-Altering

It's hard to imagine what life would have been like and who I would have become if my childhood foundations had not resulted in skewed thought patterns. I imagine there would have been much less struggle and angst.

As a little girl, wishing I was in a normal family became an unrelenting yearning. Even as an adult, I found myself jealous of people who had strong, wonderful, and married parents. I know now that even in the best of families, children experience foundational cracks, albeit some experience more of them than others. No family is perfect. The degree to which our foundations are faulty will directly affect how far off course our lives can become. The further our normal growth and development are distorted, the greater we veer from our destiny.

What destiny? We have a destiny? Yes. Many people believe we are just a product of our environment with no specific design or purpose, making our way through life and creating our own purpose. I, however, do not. Psalm 139:13–14 clearly teaches us that we are "fearfully and wonderfully made" and that God forms us with a unique purpose while we are still in our mother's womb. We further learn from Ephesians 2:10 that we were created by God for good works that have been planned in advance.

I remember the first time I read Psalm 139 as an adult. At the time, I had no idea about faulty foundations or thought patterns. The words leapt off the page and cut through my heart and its poorly erected protective walls. Although it wasn't until years later when I learned about dismantling wrong thought patterns, a seed was planted by God. I was loved and had a purpose. Do you know you are loved and that God has created you with a destiny—a destiny to uniquely bear His image?

> **Do you know you are loved, and God has created you with a destiny? A destiny to uniquely bear His image.**

My next questions would then be "What happened?" and "Why didn't I know I had a destiny?"

Sadly, Satan hates us as much as God loves us. Satan hates us solely because he hates God and wants to hurt God by hurting us. What is his plan? His plan is to veer us off course and deter us from fulfilling our divine destiny.

Like any opponent, Satan has a counterplan to thwart God's purpose in our lives. He uses people, circumstances, and experiences to take us out of alignment with God's love and truth.[8] How does he do it? He does it in one powerful way: he uses faulty foundations and entrenched, erroneous thought patterns to alter the course of our destiny.

Remember how I lost my voice because of abuse and threats? The Enemy's plan was to keep me from finding my voice and fulfilling the destiny God had for me, leaving me stuck and held captive by the flawed foundations and thought patterns he had established. The Enemy's plan for your life is the same—to thwart divine destiny.

Saving Grace: Good Memories amid Crumbling Foundations

I am so glad my life was not just filled with misformed and crumbling foundations. There were so many things that shined light in between the dark cracks. Celebrating the good of my story helps take the sting out of my history of inflicted wounds.

It has taken me years to mine the gold of my past. For many years, I felt only the pain and angst. Thankfully, I can now clearly see the gifts God graced my life with, allowing me to realize that my foundations weren't completely disintegrating.

First, God quite literally spared the lives of my brother and me. My mother wrestled with aborting my brother Doug. I'm so blessed he didn't, as he's dearly loved; but if she had, who knows if I would be here? Only God could have given my mother the inner fortitude to face life in the 1950s as a single mom with two illegitimate children and raise the four of us. Despite my mother having so many wounds, and essentially being a little girl in an adult body, she never wavered in her love and devotion for us "sibs." Her execution wasn't perfect, but she did the best she could with the tools she was given.

Secondly, I had many loving people in my life. I spent a lot of time with my maternal grandparents. Their home in Nantucket symbolized all that I loved and desired in life. They welcomed us with open arms, helping us feel loved and safe.

Every summer we visited, my grandmother covered our beds with an assortment of new outfits to bless us. Growing up with my mom's limited finances, this was like a second Christmas to us.

My beloved Gran was always nearby to talk to. Often when she was lying on the couch reading a book, she would call out, "Doosie [her pet name for me], come tell me all the dirt." In other words, she wanted to hear all the gossip that was flying around the neighborhood. We talked for hours. She gave me the attention my young heart craved.

Besides Gran and Pops, there were a few other shining lights in my life. There were beloved Sarah and Letty, and my dad's mom, Nana, who each soaked me in love. There were also other people who touched my life in one form or another. All of the teachers and staff of our elementary school, The School in Rose Valley, did an amazing job loving and caring for our family.

The school became a tight-knit family to us, and although my personal family circumstances caused rejection by a few of the students and their families, that was not the prevailing sentiment. During my early years of chaos, the school was a lifesaving buoy keeping me afloat.

Thirdly, our parents and school community provided many experiences that shaped us into individuals who would value, honor, and champion all types of people. They appreciated all cultures and treated individuals with respect, always advocating for those with challenges.

I remember hanging out at National Association for the Advancement of Colored People (NAACP) meetings where my mother was president, as well as picketing outside a crowded local garage where black

Americans were being held because the jails were overwhelmed. As a six-year-old, I was indelibly marked seeing all those faces peering out through the windows. I didn't understand why anyone would be treated like this. These experiences and others that my parents exposed us to impacted me enormously and served to teach me the value of all people.

The life we lived was filled with crazy contrasts, enabling me to have a semblance of comfort in various milieus. My mother struggled financially, but because of her privileged background, she tried to keep things nice for us.

With Dad, however, Doug's and my experience was the antithesis. We lived in a quasi-habitable old chicken coop. Although there were a few redeeming things about living with Dad, the coop with no heat or bathroom was not one of them.

Additionally, my mother's wealthy extended family provided other extremes. I'll never forget visiting Uncle Lefty in his mansion, playing in his gardens and massive library, and being pampered and doted on by his staff. It was there I learned how a formal dinner was held, which table utensils to use and when, and how to tip my soup bowl so that I could properly enjoy it to the last drop. All these experiences, from rags to riches, made me adaptable in most situations.

Finally, I am forever grateful that my mom and Bernie moved our family to Martha's Vineyard. Despite separation from my dad (which ended up being a good thing), Martha's Vineyard became a safe haven for me during the remainder of my childhood. My teen years were still filled with challenges, but being there helped me feel secure, provided family and good friends, and impacted me with many life-shaping activities—especially the two choral groups I participated in. A love of singing, passed down from my parents (and a gift from God), became this high schooler's lifeblood. Being a part of the Vineyard and its high school communities was a source of joy to my unknowingly muddled and crushed heart.

These saving graces that impacted my early years were unearthed after intense reflection and exploration of my life's faulty foundation. As much as I would like to testify that the gifts outweighed the challenges, I can't do so—but I can testify that they certainly counterbalanced them. These gifts God placed in my life enabled me to function and to appear to be somewhat normal. However, I didn't fully realize what was underneath the carefully placed veneer: a foundation that was crumbling and not sturdy enough to pass the test of time.

Have you identified at all with my brief, but vulnerable, synopsis of a chaotic childhood? For me, that childhood foundation was poor at best. Carried by that poor foundation, I moved into the formative teenage years. I pray that in the following pages you will find hope that your foundation can be restored. Despite conventional wisdom, your foundation can be rebuilt.

Chapter 3

Found in Christ

*For the Son of Man came
to seek and to save the lost.*
Luke 19:10

I never cease to be amazed at the resiliency of children in continuing
to live life in spite of traumas and detrimental experiences. God has
given mankind the amazing ability to withstand physical and emotional traumas (often by burying or repressing them) so they can continue
to function.

While traveling in Africa, I saw many children who had been abused
and/or suffered great family loss due to the HIV epidemic who were
laughing and playing while continuing to engage in life despite the traumas they experienced. I marveled that they appeared so normal.

As astounding as it was to me, I realized that I did it too. Somehow,
despite all the chaos that reigned in my young life and the crumbled
foundation that was laid, I continued to act "normal," even though I had
no idea what normal was.

As a little girl, I did what many people do: I became an accomplished
people watcher. What else was there to do while sitting for hours late at
night in the backroom of a bar with adults drinking, eating, and partying?
It was my first foray into being a true student, and wow, did I study hard
in an attempt to figure out what normal looked like! As one might expect,
normality was a tough subject to study since its meaning is so subjective.

However, I did my best. I studied people, watched television shows, read books, and even internalized the fairy tales read to all little children. Each observation became my informant for living life. As a little girl, I had no idea that the information base I formed by observation was as faulty as my foundation and as erroneous as my deeply seated thought patterns.

I sought to live my interpretation of a normal life, a fairy-tale life where it's all happiness, joy, love, laughter, and togetherness.

Armed with this information that became my internal compass, I sought to live my interpretation of a normal life—a fairy-tale life where it's all happiness, joy, love, laughter, and togetherness . . . the real happily ever after—the life that is always beckoning but is not really obtainable.

I am actually convinced that God has hardwired each of us not to yearn for the fairy tale in this life but what was lost in the beginning: heaven on earth. Unfortunately, no matter how hard I tried, life—normal life, the joyful, love- and truth-filled, satisfying life—was elusive. Despite giving all appearances of being normal, my life was anything but normal. Being honest with myself brought this realization into focus.

My life was haunted and plagued by a lonely, abandoned, insecure, and lost little girl who, unbeknownst to me, was deeply embedded in my subconscious. She was voiceless to others; nevertheless, her unrelenting impact on me made normalcy difficult to maintain. Consequently, my life was more like a series of roller-coaster rides with exhilarating highs and plummeting lows.

Lost in the Miry Pit

Ugh! I know many people love the thrill of roller coasters, but I have been trained to dislike them. As a child, I experienced the ups and downs of my mom's mothering, which included her unpredictable emotions and her delightful creativity and nurturing. Then there were the shattering hostilities between my parents that exploded without warning. Not surprisingly, to create a sense of safety, I learned to vigilantly observe my surroundings and diligently work to keep everyone around me happy and peaceful, thereby (hopefully) fending off any eruptions. I wanted to keep things stable and on an even keel. As long as I could do this, I felt safe and thought all was well with the world— at least momentarily, until the next unforeseen flare-up.

Nope. Stability was definitely not something I was acquainted with. It is no wonder I was not a fan of roller coasters; life itself was enough of a roller coaster for me.

The highs and lows propelled me into my teenage and young adult years, but by then they were more than just an external ride—they were an internalized way of life. I learned during the formative years that activities and relationships could propel me to the highs, while my background, wounds, and life experiences could just as easily plunge me to the lows. I didn't realize at the time that my childhood had left deeply embedded embers of pain in my heart that would smolder and flare up into flames anytime life's circumstances proved challenging to me. Keeping busy with friends and activities in order to battle the loneliness and hurt that accosted me at home became a never-ending cycle to try to prevent the painful embers from bursting into flame.

Most people were unaware of this internal battle because they only saw the facade I presented to the world—a facade that was happy, warm, compassionate, fun, and secure. Honestly, it wasn't all a facade. Those things do describe me, but maintaining it all the time required enormous amounts of energy so people would not see the other part of me—the undesirable part— the fearful, lonely, hopeless, and depressive part that threatened to bubble up.

Although my mother was the trained actress, I think I became quite gifted in my own right, with life being my ever-ready instructor. There were only a precious few people who were privy to my darker side, since unconsciously, rejection and isolation were always the pervasive fears knocking at the door of my heart. Therefore, I was completely committed to having my emotional veneer remain firmly in place, allowing me to project a semblance of normalcy, albeit at the cost of great emotional effort.

As I write this, I find it providential that I am vacationing on Martha's Vineyard and remembering those days gone by. I am flooded with memories and the awareness that living here was a privilege—a lifesaver. Those years hold such dear treasures that I've cherished and packed away securely in my heart: memories of singing my heart out in select choral groups, prized times with friends and family laughing and playing together, learning to be a team member on the tennis team, swimming and riding the waves at the beach, and exploring and being a part of a community. I can't go very long while visiting without remembering so many deeply loved and cherished memories, all of which shaped me and kept me safe. I am so thankful to call this place home.

Longing for this to be the only aspect of my story, I find that even now I have to willfully not linger on the highs but must allow the other side, the low side, the side of me that felt so lost and alone here, to be equally remembered. Oh, it wasn't the place, but it was the home, the family circumstance, and the background. I loved my family dearly, but the pervasive feeling of those years was of being alone and on my own—of trying to figure out life and yet having few tools or support to do it with.

> I find even now I have to willfully not linger on the highs but allow the other side, the low side, to be equally remembered.

Whatever I wanted to do, whether activities associated with school, friends, or church, I was on my own to figure it out. Rarely would my mom or stepdad attend activities at school or engage in what I was doing. They would occasionally attend a concert or musical, but they never saw me play on the tennis team. They were too involved in their own lives.

Home life was spent in my little room sleeping, singing along to music, doing homework, and reading romance novels—anything that would fill my time and keep those feelings of loneliness, and that lonely little girl, at bay.

We lived in a small, unfinished A-frame cottage in the woods—not one of those fancy homes you may have seen that are visited by presidents. With our home being less than opulent and the family dynamics being challenging, my constant companions were embarrassment and shame, which discouraged me from friendships outside of school, thereby heightening my loneliness. There were certainly pleasurable times, such as when my siblings were home or my parents' friends came over, but in my mind, these seemed few and far between.

Heading off to nursing school, I was filled with excitement to be moving toward my goals, but I was also a bit apprehensive to be leaving the relative safety of home. Since I was coming from a small island, my nursing school in a small, rural, New Hampshire college town was perfect, and I loved it.

It didn't take me long to realize that I disliked the scene and mentality of college nightlife with the drinking and carousing. It seemed so superficial to me. I attribute this and my lack of desire to indulge as a positive by-product of having an alcoholic father. There were so many other things to do, and there were many friendships that were meaningful.

My life seemed full, and it took on a busy rhythm of school, work, and friends. It was manageable, though, despite the roller-coaster ride of emotions that continued to nag at me, especially with relational challenges.

I remember times when I took emotional dives, and as often happens, they involved a certain guy. This guy had a way of toying with me and giving me mixed signals. I think I was his pet project.

I can still remember the confusion and angst this relationship caused. His flirtations and attention had the ability to bring me as high as the clouds, but his neglect (or flirtations with others) caused me to nosedive into the pit of dejection. I imagine many people have fallen prey to this type of ruthlessness and have experienced the emotional roller coaster of thrill, confusion, and despair. It can be devastating.

I am so thankful that during my years of nurse's training, my sister and her boyfriend, Ben, lived fairly close by. They were often a source of strength and support, not only during the highs, but also during the lows when I was overwhelmed. The pattern throughout the years of relational highs and lows, with their consequential emotional ride, was not something I was fully cognizant of or understood. The highs were wonderful and made it seem like all was well with the world, but the lows were another story and were difficult to climb out of, leaving me feeling lost, alone, and hopeless.

Have you ever felt that your life was a series of patterns developed to keep an equilibrium in your life, only to find that these same patterns don't always work—and subsequently you experience exhilarating highs and agonizing lows? I found this challenging, and that is why I attempted to maintain an even keel with minimal emotional roller coasters.

Once I Was Lost, but Now I Am Found

There was one particular low I just couldn't climb out of. It had to do with another guy. I met him in the summer between my junior and senior years in nursing school when we were both working at a 4-H camp on Martha's Vineyard. Jimmy, an off-islander, was working as the camp swimming instructor, and I had the good fortune to be his assistant. What ensued was an amazing summer fling—the kind you see in the movies.

We had so much fun flirting and frolicking in the water together. I'm not sure if those little campers received much swim instruction with Jimmy and me so enthralled with each other. That summer was easily one of the most amazing summers of my young adult life. I was soaring high with my head in the clouds.

As it always does, summer came to an end, and with it came our parting for separate schools. We gave each other well-intentioned promises to stay in touch and to see each other at the first possible opportunity.

Despite coming off such an exhilarating summer experience, along with my sadness over missing Jimmy, I returned to school as a senior with great excitement. However, the days with no word from Jimmy turned into weeks, and the weeks turned into months. I received no response to my phone calls or letters. Radio silence. Zip. Nada. It was as if the whole summer had been a dream.

Being completely naïve and innocent in matters of relationships, I couldn't understand what in the world had happened. I know now that summer flings are simply that—summer flings. At the time though, I didn't know. With all of the girlfriends my dad had, I suppose I should have known better, but I really had no clue.

The crash came very forcefully. All the questions continually swirled in my head as I tried to figure out what went wrong, What did I do? Why did he completely cut me off and reject me? How could he do such a thing after we had so much fun?

With each cycle of the questions and no possibility of answers, I emotionally spiraled deeper and deeper into despair and confusion. I just couldn't understand. As was my pattern with relationships, whether male or female, I made it about me. I was the problem. I was the defect. There was something wrong with me. Projecting the blame onto myself was a destructive pattern that directly pointed back to my faulty foundation and mindset.

Making it through the fall semester with the busyness of school was only accomplished by my drivenness to overachieve, the help of precious friends, and a sheer act of will.

Christmas break allowed a trip home for the holidays, which swallowed me up with memories of the summer and left me feeling more dejected and alone. I was in a pit that I had no idea how to climb out of.

Returning to school for the last months of training before graduation, I couldn't shake the hopelessness I felt. For some reason, I turned to my older brother Tony. He had been talking to me for a few years about some religious transformation he had, and although at the time I didn't understand why, I felt the need to talk to him about it. I intuitively knew he had the answer I needed.

Tony connected me to the Christian fellowship group that met on the college campus, and I went to the first service I could. It was there, that night, that I heard about Jesus. As a result, I gave my heart to Him with a simple prayer. I didn't really understand what it all meant, but I knew I needed Jesus, and what was shared of the gospel made sense to me. Jesus captured my heart with His love that night.

I didn't really understand what it all meant, but I knew I needed Jesus, and what they shared about the gospel made sense.

I was a different person than who I was before the service. The hopelessness and despair were gone. I was filled with joy. It seemed as if I were soaring. I had no clue what had happened, but I knew something had. I told everyone I could about it. They did not really understand, because even I didn't understand, but there was no denying the change in me. My friends were thrilled.

I marvel at the incredible timing of God. Within a week after giving my life to the Lord, I met my future husband—yup, that handsome medical student. Within a month, we were dating. Talk about highs! I had met Jesus and had given my life to Him, I was in my final months of nursing school, I was attending Bible studies, and I was dating my handsome Johnny. My mourning had certainly turned into dancing (Psalm 30:11).

With the end of school rapidly approaching, I made the decision to move to Pennsylvania for my first nursing position. As a new Christian, I could then be near Tony and his new bride, Jami, and I could attend their church. My relationship with John continued to blossom, but with our romance still in its infancy, it was too soon to make future plans together. Besides, a medical student's residency assignments were dependent on the match system, so John had no control over where he would go. By the end of March, John found out he was headed to Syracuse, New York, for his resident training.

That spring prior to graduation was glorious, and it was so much more than I had ever experienced. I was dating and falling in love with John, I was walking with Jesus and experiencing fellowship with other believers, and I was finishing nurse's training. Life was good.

That summer, John and I went our separate ways. Being a bit wiser after my hurtful experience from the summer before, I wasn't sure how our relationship would turn out. This time, though, I was armed with the faith that Jesus was with me, and I leaned into trusting Him for my future.

Tony and Jami were loving supports. They helped me get involved in their church, buy my first car, find delightful Christian roommates, and essentially take my first steps as an adult in the real world. The days (and nights) became filled with my first nursing job, time with Tony and Jami, church activities, and spending every other weekend traveling to visit John.

Despite John's demanding internship, our relationship continued to grow. There were a few people in the church, however, who were definitely against my relationship with John. He was not an overt, outspoken Christian, and I was told that we were unequally yoked. Being new to the faith, I didn't really get it. Loving him and having a deep sense that I would marry him, I definitely wasn't inclined to push him away.

Looking back on that time, I am so grateful for the footing it gave me. More importantly, I am grateful for the precious time I had with Tony and Jami. However, it was also a time in which great conflict developed within me about faith. This was partially my own fault, and partially the fault of the church.

First, in full disclosure, the personal conflict was regarding premarital sex. Being a Christian even for a short time, I knew that sex before marriage was wrong biblically. However, the sexual lifestyle of my parents, along with the deeply entrenched message of "You can't say no" (instilled from being sexually abused), warred against this new conviction—and it won.

My personal choices about intimacy with John weighed deeply on my heart and placed the beginnings of a wedge between the Lord and me. Deep down, I knew it was wrong, but I was so much in love, and my subconscious lessons from my early childhood told me I would be rejected if I made any other choice.

Unfortunately, around the same time, other circumstances and the behavior of church leaders became very confusing and hurtful to me. This drove the wedge deeper and separated me further from church. With John's prompting, I joined him in Syracuse, and we were engaged shortly after.

Although living with John was a joy, it heightened my internal conflict about living in sin. As a result, I pulled away from the church and from fellowship with other believers. Although I never stopped believing

> I placed myself in the driver's seat of my life and relegated Jesus to the backseat.

in Jesus, my life became more about pursuing happiness with John than pleasing God. Essentially, I placed myself in the driver's seat of my life and relegated Jesus to the back seat.

A year after our graduation, John and I returned to Martha's Vineyard to be married. We made our vows before God, which, forty-two years later, we still hold as sacred. Once married, I embarked on an adventure with the love of my life, leaving my challenging background behind once and for all. I reached for the happily ever after I had read so much about.

Don't you wish it were that easy?

Roadblocks Lead to Surrender

How I loved being married! I got to be with my best friend every day. The first few years of marriage were fantastic. We spent our time exploring, traveling, working, playing, moving for John's medical training, and setting up our first two homes. Life was good—with a blend of togetherness, pursuing our own career dreams, and beginning a family.

Becoming a mother was a delight. I fully loved exploring the world with our first son, Matthew. John enjoyed the time he had with us, but the rigors of training made family times few and far between. Looking back, I definitely see that the relational roadblocks from our childhood experiences—wounds neither of us knew existed—appeared in these early years of marriage.

At this point, with John's all-consuming medical training and my background, my independence began to show. My unresolved issues with male abusers had caused me to make a subconscious vow to never again let men overpower me or tell me what to do. This often came across as an undercurrent of stubbornness and rebellion toward John, which was not exactly conducive to a healthy relationship.

Between his pursuit of medical training and the need to add extra income with a second job, John's time was eaten up, leaving little for me. This set off a series of all too familiar mental messages from my past, such as, "I'm not worth his time," "He loves work more than me," "I'm not valuable," and "I'm all alone."

John never intended to send these messages. Although declaring that he always liked my feistiness, my discontent—often expressed in anger—was not appreciated. It only served to make him retreat or maybe to head back to work a little bit earlier than necessary.

My emotional and relational roadblocks surfaced and seemed to get in the way of my dreams, no matter how unrealistic the dreams were. They worked against me and blocked me from all that I desired. That was how I felt anyway, and I was miserable and filled with pain.

I finally couldn't stand it any longer, so I insisted that John and I go to counseling. Maybe a counselor could remove the roadblocks so we could have smooth sailing again. Thankfully, John was as committed to me as I was to him, and he agreed to go.

As often happens in life, pain motivated me to reach out to Jesus in faith, in addition to the counseling. We were attending a church as a family, wanting our son to be raised in the church. However, it missed something and served more as a social club for us.

So what do I do when I don't know what to do? As before, I called my brother Tony, who at this point was attending a Bible school. He faithfully pointed me once again in the direction of a Bible-believing church, and it was there that I rededicated my life to God and was filled with the Holy Spirit.

John didn't understand, and our counselor explained that my turning to faith was an overreaction to John being at work all the time. But I knew the truth. I needed Jesus in the driver's seat of my life if I was ever going to have a successful marriage, be a successful mother, and have a successful life. I knew that surrendering my heart completely to Him was the only way to true life for me, so I asked Christ to become Lord of my life. The joy that I had received from Him years before returned. With prayer, Johnny gave his life to Christ soon after, and our adventure in faith together began.

The Perfect Life?

By the time we had been married six years and had our second son, Christopher, John and I had moved four times. Little did I know that this would be a career trend. I was oblivious to the demands placed upon an academic physician with years of training. Frequent moves and long hours of dedication were required to advance John's career, often leaving me seemingly a single mom raising our three precious children alone.

We lived with a beeper that went off at all hours, calling John away regardless of whether he was sleeping, at our son's birthday party, or on a desperately needed date with me. I had gone into marriage to a doctor blindly armed with only my idealized hopes and dreams.

Even so, I wouldn't have changed it because I was with my love, John, and God knew what He was doing when He brought us together. We are so different, yet we value and enjoy so many of the same things. No, I wouldn't have chosen some of these facets of our life, yet I am very grateful for them because our life together, with Christ at the helm, has been quite an adventure—one God has used to heal me and point me back to the destiny He intended.

Our move to Richmond for John's first "real" job (this was how I teased him, as he had been working and training exhaustively for the prior six years) as an attending physician was one I call foundational. We were still new Christians, and we found an amazing church where we could become involved and grow—singing on the worship team, leading a Sunday school class, and helping to serve in whatever capacity was needed. These years were full, with two little boys, dear friends to walk through life with, job requirements, and visits with family to stay in touch.

But there were rumblings from my crumbled foundations—feelings of insecurity that I wasn't good enough.

However, there were also rumblings from my crumbled foundation—feelings of insecurity that I wasn't good enough. I countered these rumblings with the busyness of life, and I seemed to be fairly successful at it. Unfortunately, its efficacy proved temporary.

Just before the birth of our third child, Caitlin, we moved to Cleveland, Ohio, for a new position. John was recruited to be the director of the Cardiac Catheterization Lab. It was quite an honor, and John was beginning to be recognized in his field.

From start to finish, the move was an act of faith, even down to the specific house we bought. The following years were filled with busy, energetic children, serving our church in the children's ministry, directing the church Christmas plays, developing dear lifelong friendships, attending Bible studies, and exploring and experiencing the delights of Cleveland.

Did I mention children, children, and children? John was stretched to the max with work, work, and more work, with a little family involvement and service to church mixed in. We lived in a big, beautiful turn-of-the-century home that was decorated in a fashion my grandmother would have approved of. We had two vehicles (one of them a minivan, of course) and a beloved family golden retriever. I loved my husband, my children, our friends, our church, and everything about my life. I was living the dream!

But if I was living the dream, why did I have that family picture I previously mentioned where I looked like an ice queen—a picture in which everyone was perfectly placed and dressed?

Sadly, I now realize that I was living the dream that was created out of the wounds and dysfunction of my background. I worked tirelessly to orchestrate this perfect life fashioned after my perception of my grandmother's life: normal and filled with happiness. Yes, I had the perfect life and the perfect family. I had successfully created the dream. People even proclaimed it. We were the perfect family and had the perfect life.

There was only one problem, and that picture revealed it: I had no happiness. Gratitude yes, but happiness and joy? No.

There was only one problem, and that picture revealed it: I had no happiness. Yes, I had much gratitude, but I did not have happiness and joy. It was such a confusing place to be. I was at a complete loss, and I kept asking the Lord what was wrong with me. Having years of Bible study under my belt, I knew I was not living the abundant life that Jesus promised believers in Scripture. Something wasn't right.

It was at this low point of my life when I cried out to the Lord and told Him He had to do something. I was not moving forward in my walk with Him. I was reading one thing in the Bible and experiencing another. He had to do something!

Well, He did do something, and it was nothing I could have ever imagined: He led me to reopen and reexamine my painful childhood.

Prayer for Salvation

As you read this chapter, maybe you feel a tug on your heart to surrender your life to the Lord Jesus Christ. That tug is Christ's Spirit knocking at the door of your heart.

The Bible tells us that if we respond and open the door with a simple prayer said from the sincerity of our heart, Jesus will come in and commune with us (Revelation 3:20).

Romans 10:9–10 assures us that "if you confess with your mouth that Jesus is Lord and believe in your heart that God raised him from the dead, you will be saved. For with the heart one believes and is justified, and with the mouth one confesses and is saved." This means that as you say the prayer, you will be saved. You might want to pray this out loud, for we know from the Bible that faith comes from hearing (Romans 10:17). Jesus hears our prayer, and He is the only one who has the power to save us through faith in His finished work on the cross.

For those who desire, I have included a simple prayer for you to recite.[9]

Prayer of Salvation

> Father, I know that I have broken Your laws and that my sins have separated me from You. I am truly sorry, and now I want to turn away from my past sinful life and turn toward You. Please forgive me and help me to avoid sinning again. I believe that Your Son, Jesus Christ, died for my sins, was resurrected from the dead, is alive, and hears my prayer. I invite Jesus to become the Lord of my life, to rule and reign in my heart from this day forward. Please send Your Holy Spirit to help me obey You and to do Your will for the rest of my life. In Jesus's name, I pray. Amen.

Welcome to the family of God! If you sincerely prayed this prayer and placed your faith in Jesus Christ alone, you are now a follower of Christ and an adopted child of God.

Salvation doesn't depend on a feeling, but it is a very real spiritual transaction that occurs in response to your faith and declaration. In order to grow in your faith, I would encourage you to begin by reading the book of John in the Bible and finding a local Christian church to attend.

Part 2

Uncovering
and
Dismantling
Captivity

Chapter 4

Courage to Face
the Truth

*And you will know the truth,
and the truth will set you free.*
John 8:32

When I got married, I distinctly turned the page and closed the book once and for all on the craziness of my childhood. That was what I thought, anyway. I'd had enough, and I wanted to completely embrace my new life as an adult, nurse, and wife.

This didn't mean that I would turn my back on my family and leave them in the dust of my marriage vows, for I loved them too much. Nevertheless, it did mean I would forge ahead, forgetting what was behind and making all my dreams come true. That was biblical, right? Paul tells us to forget what lies behind and strain forward to what lies ahead (Philippians 3:13).

Years into my life as a wife and mother, I thought I was pretty good at this. Imagine my surprise when I found myself living the dream, yet falling flat on my face and feeling dead inside. Well, that's not completely true. I had a few feelings, such as happiness when others were around. Generally, though, I was plagued with feelings of being overwhelmed, underequipped, insecure, and a complete failure at being a wife and a mother. And of course, there were the ever-present feelings of anger lurking just below the surface ready to lash out at a moment's notice.

I found myself stuck, wanting so much more for my children, yet feeling utterly incapable of being healthier no matter how hard I tried. It was at this point that I began crying out to the Lord, not only saying, *Help, Lord! What should I do?* but adding the perpetual *I'm sorry* because of my failure to Him.

I recognized that what I had abhorred, I had unknowingly become.

I had failed Him, I had failed my husband, and in my mind, I had definitely failed my children. My propensity to flare up with them reminded me of none other than my mother. As a child, I had vowed never to be like her—never to treat my children the way she had treated me. Then I recognized that what I had abhorred, I had unknowingly become. It simply made no sense to me. I literally had everything I could ever want—or that was what I thought, anyway.

We have already established that asking God a question will definitely bring an answer. I can't completely remember the specifics of how God answered, but I know I made the decision to go to counseling, and I prayed He would direct me to someone who could expose my problem and put me back on the path to happiness.

It's laughable as I look back at my ignorance. Not understanding the journey to wholeness and sanctification I was about to embark on, I thought there was some quick fix to my problem. However, God, true to His loving nature and despite my ignorance, guided this broken woman, His daughter, to a loving Christian counselor who had walked the same path. God gently placed me in her care and tenderly began to unravel the truth that only He knew was bound deep within my broken heart.

Thus, the journey began!

Saying Yes to God

I felt incredulous at that first counseling appointment. As the counselor queried me about my background, I easily rattled off the data with precision. When she pulled out her chart that depicted pictures of different emotions and asked me how I felt, I was dumbfounded. First, I couldn't believe there were so many emotions—at least thirty were pictured. Secondly, I had no idea how I felt. It was as if my head had been cut off from my heart and was relaying painful history with minimal, if any, emotions.

I didn't know this was abnormal. How could I know that closing the door on trauma and painful experiences didn't actually make them disappear? How could I know that stuffing all my emotions would one day separate me from what truly made me human—my heart? How could I know that unexpressed emotions would eventually burst out in unhealthy, hurtful ways as the repressed wounds were reignited by experiences smacking of similarity? Thus, the flare-ups. Nothing disappears by simply willing it away, for it inevitably leaks out in one form or another—generally in a negative way. I didn't know that then.

> **How could I know that closing the door on trauma and painful experiences didn't actually make them disappear?**

Several months into therapy, I had a session that forever changed my life. I can't remember anything that I was talking about, but I will never forget the counselor's response. She asked, "Do you think you might have been sexually abused?"

The question shook me. "What do you mean?" I asked, stunned.

She proceeded to explain her thoughts. Of course, I knew that my dad's behavior and having pornography around wasn't quite normal, but at the time I didn't realize the impact it had had on me. However, she felt there was more. I was completely blank. I knew I had experienced some abnormal things, but sexual abuse? Wouldn't I remember?

She assured me that many people don't remember their abuse because it is so painful that they repress it. I left her office that day completely conflicted. On the one hand, I didn't want to deny anything, but on the other hand, I didn't want someone to make suggestions that were not true. At the time, there was a big hubbub about counselors making suggestions and their clients believing those suggestions falsely.

I didn't want any part of that.

Me being me, I went back to the Lord and started querying Him. *Is this true, Lord? I only want the truth! You know the truth, Lord, and I don't want anything to do with things that are false or deceptive.*

Honestly, I was in so much angst that I continually cried out, *I just want truth, Lord!* God's Word became such a comfort to me at this time because, although I didn't feel it, I was assured that God listens to the cries of His children (Psalm 145:18–19). According to the Hebrew, this means that God actually bends down to hear our prayers.

Oh, did I need that at that moment, with my heart in a constant state of turmoil! It was at that point that I heard a still, small voice say, "You will know the truth, and the truth will set you free" (John 8:32). It was just the assurance I needed to quiet my tumultuous heart, and it was the promise I clung to for years.

Over the next few months, I read everything I could about sexual abuse. At that time, there really weren't many Christian resources, so I pored over the secular ones. It became hard to deny that I had experienced a lot of what was described in these books and had lived through many of the examples that were given. Even though the Lord had promised that I would know the truth, I still wasn't convinced that I had been sexually abused.

I decided to take a summer trip with the kids and circle the northeast, visiting my siblings on a discovery mission. I wanted their thoughts about this new possibility looming over my head. I especially looked forward to talking with Doug, as he and I shared many of the same experiences and had a special, loving bond together.

I came away from that trip finally able to accept the reality: it was highly probable that I had been sexually abused at a very young age.

Doug had many memories relating to the abuse, some of which he shared. Since I had specifically asked, he felt more free to confirm my suspicions; however, he wouldn't share details. He explained that when I was ready, I would remember them myself. I wasn't so sure. I had a difficult enough time even accepting the details he did share. But my trust was in God, and He promised that I would know the truth.

Once I was home, I continued to process this new truth, and I found myself feeling devastated. I knew my life wasn't normal, but to now face this new reality that I had been sexually abused as a young girl, and had repressed it so completely, was too much. Where was my mom? Why did she let this happen, and how could it have happened anyway? Where was my dad? Was he, as my brother professed, complicit?

I was overwhelmed. I shared my feelings with my counselor: "I can't cry because, seriously, I think once I start, I won't ever stop!" I could see no way out. I was going down into the pit and was never coming out.

That was when the second part of John 8:32 hit me: the truth would set me free. I knew that I wanted freedom. It seemed there was only one way to it—the journey to truth.

At that moment, I perceived the Lord offering me a choice. His way is to offer and never force. He is ever gentle and kind. The choice for this journey was mine. I could say yes, or I could say no.

I intuitively knew that if I said yes to this journey, there would be suffering. I was reminded of Christ's suffering on the cross. I'm convinced He was reticent to take the journey to the cross,

> I intuitively knew that if I said yes to this journey, there would be suffering.

which He knew would include incredible suffering. Scripture hints at His wrestling between "no" and "yes" when it records His words, "My Father, if it be possible, let this cup pass from me" (Matthew 26:39).

Yet we see in Hebrews that Jesus endured the cross, the suffering, for a greater purpose. He was able to look past the suffering and see the joy on the other side—the freedom for Himself, for me, and for you (Hebrews 12:2). In the end, Jesus said, "Not as I will, but as you will" (Matthew 26:39).

It struck me that the way of suffering was also the way of resurrection to freedom and new life in Christ. In the past, this concept had been alien to me, and suffering was to be avoided at all costs. However, I now saw that this journey to freedom and truth would involve suffering for a time, but in the end, it would lead me to what I deeply yearned for—freedom in Christ.

With this realization, I wholeheartedly said yes to Jesus, fully committing myself to the journey He had placed before me. Since that time, seeing Christ's faithfulness to bring me through the journey, I have adopted the saying, "Just say yes!" If you find yourself at a point of decision with Christ, I want to encourage you to say yes to Jesus, for He will be faithful to you just as He was to me.

Saying Goodbye to Hypocrisy

With the decision solidified within me, I purposed to embrace all that Jesus wanted to do in and through me. I didn't know where the journey would take me, but I was committed to follow every dip and turn, every crooked, twisted, and low path the Lord would take me on.

> I purposed to embrace all that Jesus wanted to do in and through me.

One of the biggest challenges for me was the realization that I would be alone on much of this journey since my husband, friends, and church leaders and members didn't understand what I was going through. It was as if I were speaking to them in a foreign language whenever I tried to share the journey. It is such an isolating experience; at the time, few people in Christian circles had heard about this type of inner healing.

Leaders didn't know what to do with me. More often than not, they would quote either 2 Corinthians 5:17 or Philippians 3:13, and then they would kindly explain to me that I was a new creation in Christ, all these past things were gone, and I needed to forget them. I didn't find this helpful. It only served to create doubt in my heart about whether or not I was on the right path.

It was not that I doubted the validity of these Bible verses, but they reignited my angst. Maybe I was being led astray and these leaders were right. Maybe I was desperately flawed and unable to perceive God.

These early days were incredibly challenging to me because I felt as if I were a lone fish trying to swim upstream against a strong current. Every time someone looked at me as if I were crazy, or if they quoted Scripture to me (I'm sure they had good intentions of turning me back to the right direction of the current), I felt more and more isolated and more like a misfit. The doubts and feelings of insecurity washed over me, leading me to question whether I was walking deeper into deception, or if the Lord was really leading me into freedom. It was painful enough to relive and get in touch with my broken heart, let alone doing it among external indicators that I was missing it.

I am so appreciative that Jesus knew what He was doing when He sent me to my counselor. She was an incredibly supportive and loving person, always closing our time together by looking me in the eyes and saying, "I believe in you!"

> "I believe in you" . . . these words were water to my parched heart.

Those words were water to my parched heart. When I didn't know how to believe in myself, she believed in me. She served as a guide moved by the Lord's hand to lead me through the dark days of truth discovery and subsequent healing. Jesus used her and the resources she put in my hands to anchor me to His path, despite the swirling contradictory messages emanating from all around me. Sadly, most were coming from the church body.

However, I came to the place where the pressure from within and from without was too much for me to handle. My life felt completely out of control. Falling apart, with three small children to care for, was out of the question. My husband, always the supporter of anything Dinah, readily agreed when my counselor recommended that I go away for a weeklong intensive program for inner healing. I knew I had to go—not as much for myself, but for my children. I loved them so much, and everything I did was motivated by my love for them. I felt that I wasn't worth it, but I knew they definitely were.

Even the freedom I was pursuing was for them. I wanted to be the mommy they needed, and I wanted to keep them from experiencing pain like I had experienced. I would do anything for them, and I knew that what I was currently giving them was less than I had dreamed about or what was healthy for them.

Leaving my children was agonizing. They wouldn't understand. How could they? They didn't know that this was something I had to do for them. Getting better for them was what propelled me and helped me get on the plane that day more than three decades ago. It was one of the best decisions I ever made.

At the program, I learned from seasoned counselors who were well down the road on this type of journey, and they confirmed I wasn't crazy. Going forward in Christ and truly being a new creation overflowing with His Spirit meant going back and emptying myself of the junk that had resulted from a faulty foundation.

The spiritual dynamic that we are new creations when we are saved by Christ is true. Equally true is the reality that in order to fully apprehend this new spiritual reality, the old junk from our background must be cleaned out so we can be filled with His Spirit. It finally made sense to me.

That week was intense. They claimed it was like six months of counseling rolled up into one week. I met many new friends there who were on the same journey. For once, I didn't feel like such an aberration. I learned more fully how damaging dysfunctional backgrounds are, and I was encouraged to apply that information in the group sessions.

Our time there was transforming, and we each felt fully supported as we took baby steps toward honesty and truth. Many of us realized for the first time just how hypocritical our lives were. We had been wearing masks to shield the truth in an attempt to make ourselves more lovable and acceptable. These masks served to separate us from others, but surprisingly, they also separated us from ourselves.

> I promised the Lord that with His help I would turn away from my survival mode of hypocrisy and embrace a life of honesty.

Individually, we committed to shed the masks of hypocrisy and to learn to walk in truth and honesty. Understandably, this was easier said than done. However, I took that commitment seriously, and I promised the Lord that with His help I would turn away from my survival mode of hypocrisy and embrace a life of honesty. I have found this promise challenging. It is not always well received, but it is definitely the way of the Lord.

Our Emotional Indicator Signs

Embracing a life of truth left me staring squarely into the depths of my heart. At the time, I honestly couldn't see anything good in myself. I was overwhelmed by the ugliness I saw, and I couldn't see how the Lord could love someone so ugly.

Here I was, a Christian, and I still felt this way. What was wrong with me? Didn't I know what God said about me? Frankly, no! Well, I might have known it in my head, but the problem was that I didn't know it in my heart. The truth of what I knew in my head couldn't penetrate my heart because there was still so much junk in there—so many emotions not yet dealt with.

Naively, I thought that having these emotions meant I was bad. I didn't realize at the time that they were just emotions and had nothing to do with who I really was. I had learned the church messages successfully that most emotions were bad and that we should not trust them—and we definitely should not give room to them since they are sinful and will inevitably lead us astray. However, I quickly learned that "good" emotions were acceptable and godly. Not a problem!

Growing up, I had already learned the lesson of stuffing emotions well. I had learned that emotions were unsafe, caused much hurt, and weren't really tolerated by adults, so I inadvertently crammed them inside.

Once I became a Christian, I internalized the messages, allowing them to be the wall that continued to hold all the feelings—the good, the bad, and the ugly—captive and hidden away. Unfortunately, encapsulating emotions becomes an unconscious capability that lacks the discernment to be able to tell which emotions are good and allowed and which ones are bad and need to be isolated and stowed away.

I remember two specific occasions when God started teaching me the truth about emotions. The first was on a beautiful day when I was pulling weeds in our garden. That still, small voice, which I knew was the Lord's, started telling me that although I kept looking at myself, all I saw were the weeds that were covering the beauty of the plantings He had placed in me.

God continued to explain to me that I was like a beautiful garden that He had planted, and life experiences had embedded weeds and emotions in me that had nothing to do with my identity. Those weeds continued to grow, and they often seemingly overtook the flowers He had planted.

As I continued to work in the garden, God continued to nudge me. All I saw were the weeds and not the precious flowers that He saw underneath the weeds. He reassured me that these "weeds" were no problem for Him and that He could easily pull them out by the roots so they would be permanently removed.

He shared that all too often, Christians attempt to chop off the "weeds" while leaving the roots, so the weeds continue to regrow. Being a visual person, I understood this analogy and never forgot the truth of God's lesson. It took a while for this "aha" moment to completely sink in. Thankfully, God knew this and continued to underscore this truth in other ways.

Another lesson came as more of a slow dawn rising, this time while I was participating in a Bible study. This particular Bible study had us spend a lot of time in the Psalms. Over the months of the study, I was struck by how David was so real with God about his feelings. At the time, I still projected onto God the image of my angry abuser who had successfully shut me up. Coupled with faulty Christian messages about emotions, my concept of God had me bound in fear, thinking that if I had "bad" emotions, God would drop a big sledgehammer down from heaven and destroy me. It's really sad that this was how I felt about God, but it is common for us to project our earthly experiences with authority figures onto Him.

In any case, the Bible study revealed how real David was. Considering that God called him "a man after his own heart" (1 Samuel 13:14), I was moved that God was not afraid of, or upset with, David's expression of emotion.

This was truly an epiphany for me, and it solidified my understanding that emotions in and of themselves aren't bad. The words from Ephesians bounced into my heart: "Be angry and do not sin" (Ephesians 4:26). There was something to that verse. The truth erupted in my heart! It is not the emotions that are wrong or bad, but it's what we do with the emotions that makes all the difference. Emotions are just that—emotions. How we handle them is critical.

It's not the emotions that are wrong or bad, but it's what we do with the emotions that makes all the difference.

As I was driving in the car one day, God expounded on His tutorial regarding emotions. I laugh as I think back to this. Isn't that just the time when God drops a download on our hearts—when we are minding our own business and living life?

Looking at the car's dashboard, I saw the various indicator lights—those lights that light up when something is wrong with the car. I don't like those lights! I want everything to function smoothly.

In that moment, God likened the car's indicator lights to emotions; they can be warning signs, much like indicator lights. They reveal what is going on in our souls or hearts. They are not good or bad, but are simply indicators of what is happening on the inside of an individual.

When the emotions are "good," we embrace them, but when they are "bad," indicating that something is going on "under the hood," too often we ignore them. Ignoring them rather than exploring or dealing with their root cause enables emotions to result in negative behaviors.

This message really hit home for me. That was what I had been doing for so many years. I had been ignoring the emotional indicator lights that revealed that trouble was brewing. I'm so thankful that I eventually got the message and turned to God to have Him fix my broken parts.

Following a Way of Life

I hope I'm not giving the impression that we should follow emotions, people, or anything else blindly. That is not what I am endorsing, and that is not what I do in my own life. From start to finish, I am committed to following the Lord on this journey. He is the "author and finisher" of my faith (Hebrews 12:2 KJV), and He is the only One who can see me through to the end of this life's journey.

I cannot trust in myself, but I do trust His Word, which promises that "he who began a good work in you will bring it to completion at the day of Jesus Christ" (Philippians 1:6). As I follow Him, He will lead me in the way of truth and life since He is "the way, and the truth, and the life" (John 14:6).

As I follow Him, He will lead me in the way of truth and life.

Therein lies the problem, right? How do we know how to follow

Him? The answer seems simple. He'll show you! It is simple, yet it sometimes feels impossible and seems that we are following blindly.

It reminds me of when my mom and I would walk along our wooded path at night. We couldn't see anything. While walking arm in arm with me, she would frequently ask, "You on the path, Dine?"

I would generally respond, "I'm on the path, Mom. You on the path?"

If either of us were off the path, we would pull the other back on. I remember those moments fondly.

Jesus has a way of helping us follow Him as well. He helps us so we won't lose our way and fall off His path. He uses many different ways to communicate with us and guide us.

As a new Christian, I didn't have a clue that God desired, and was able, to communicate with His children. Over the years, I have discovered that God does speak. He longs to commune with people, and He does so continually. I knew God spoke through His Word—that was pretty obvious—but other than that, and me talking to Him through prayer, I didn't know how He communicated.

Once I understood that God spoke, I started fussing at Him about not being able to hear His voice. I think sometimes God just shakes His head at us and laughs. I certainly would. Thankfully, God didn't get mad and shake His fist at me. He doesn't do that. Anyway, He had another lesson in store for me.

One day when I answered the phone, I recognized the person's voice and greeted the person by name. As soon as I hung up, an inner voice spoke to me: "You recognized that person's voice on the phone after only meeting him once. Do you not think you can recognize *My* voice?"

Wow! I thought about this and realized it was true. I thanked God that He never lost patience with me and that He faithfully continued to teach me, and then I asked Him to help me recognize His voice more and more.

In addition to His Word and a quiet voice speaking to your spirit, there are many other ways in which God will speak to you and help you follow Him. One way that jumps out to me, and for which I am so grateful, is that He speaks to us through other people.

Years ago, when I was in the thick of dealing with my background (or "baggage," as I now call it), I was at a very low point and didn't know how I would have the strength to continue. While in the shower, I was sobbing and crying out to God. I was at my lowest, and I told Jesus I couldn't do it anymore.

At that moment, I heard the phone ring. Back then we didn't have cell phones. Since I had to be available in case there was an issue with my kids, I quickly got out of the shower and ran to the bedroom. Sopping wet and wrapped in a towel, I picked up the phone.

A dear friend said, "God impressed me to call you."

I don't remember anything else he said. *God impressed me to call you.* With that one call, hope was restored, and I knew somehow that the Lord would see me through the dark time. Because of my friend's obedience, I sensed the love and touch of God. It made all the difference. God saw me, heard me, and responded in love.

Sometimes God uses other people to simply encourage us, or He might have them share the wisdom we've been praying for. There have been many times in my life when God used others to encourage or guide me or give me the wisdom I was lacking. What a gift!

I'm thankful that God can't be placed in a box and that He is so creative in the ways He leads us. He can use dreams, trances, pictures, visitations, impressions, audible voices, or—as in the case of Balaam in the Bible—He can even enable a donkey to speak (Numbers 22:28). Although the Lord occasionally uses some of these ways with me, He knows I am a visual person, so He typically uses pictures, visions, or His still, small voice to speak to me.

I'm thankful God can't be placed in a box and is so creative in the ways He leads us.

One time when I was asking God what freedom would look like in my life, I instantly saw a picture in my mind's eye. I was in a field with wildflowers all around, and the sun was shining brightly. I saw myself in a white, flowing, ballerina-type gown. My long hair cascaded down my shoulders. The expression of deep, satisfying joy was written all over my upturned face.

As I looked at the picture in my mind's eye, I envisioned myself dancing freely, without inhibitions or a care in the world. This vision has remained with me and has been a source of encouragement through the years. I see myself, through Christ's leading, realizing this picture more and more. In the heart of God is a vision for your life, too, and He will use whatever means it takes to communicate with you. I'm so glad that God is for us, loves us, and—just as in the garden of Eden—wants to talk with us.

The journey of pursuing the truth is not for the faint of heart.

The journey of pursuing the truth is not for the faint of heart, and sadly, many people refuse it with a resounding "No!" They refuse to even set foot on the path the Lord wants to lead them on. Some people consent to the path initially, but as soon as they sense a challenging segment of the journey that is fraught with danger and loss of control, they veer off and choose a more comfortable, well-worn pathway.

Staying on the path takes faith, but developing that level of faith is also part of the journey. It certainly was for me!

Chapter 5

Pursuing Truth with Faith

*Do not be conformed to this world, but be trans-
formed by the renewal of your mind, that by testing
you may discern what is the will of God, what is
good and acceptable and perfect.*
Romans 12:2

Beginning an unknown journey often feels like standing all alone on a steep precipice while looking out and not seeing any clear path. You look for a place to turn as your "Yes" reverberates softly against the canyon walls of your heart.

I think of the scene in *Indiana Jones and the Last Crusade* where Indy is standing on a ledge facing a deep canyon and has to get over to the other side. I've often felt the same way. I know where I want to go, but there is a chasm between me and my destination. Any wrong step will likely send me into free fall and destruction.

I remember facing this very challenge as a little girl when I was backstage at the theater. I was attempting to climb up to see my dad in the light booth. My dilemma was that between him and me was a space with no floor and a ten-foot drop to the stage below. I was petrified looking over this breach and torn because I wanted to be with my daddy. I turned around and went back down the stairs, feeling too terrified to cross the opening.

Getting to our journey's destination can look as daunting as Indiana Jones's goal did to him, or as mine did to me as a little girl trying to get to my father. Our natural sight is often deceiving.

If we think back to the scene with Indiana Jones, we can see that there were two elements that were critical to the successful accomplishment of his goal: pursuit and faith. Indiana was determined to achieve his goal at all costs. He took a step of faith. The lifelong journey we are on requires the same kind of tenacity and faith that Indiana exemplified. These were innate attributes I felt I didn't possess.

I now realize how wrong I was. My very survival in the midst of chaos spoke a different testament. However, standing on the precipice of decision with my "Yes" solidly behind me, I knew that the healing journey before me required much more than tenacity.

Joshua, told about in the Bible, did not simply stand there and allow God to do everything for him. Taking the territory required action on his part, just as it does for us. For Joshua, pursuit was required; for us, we must pursue truth. In other words, we need to follow, chase after, strive for, and be on a quest for truth.

All these are descriptors of action. Indiana Jones couldn't just look at the other side and expect to get there. He had to act. Joshua had to bolster up courage and step out in faith, trusting that what God promised would come to pass if he first acted.

I don't always like this part. Couldn't God just do it for me? Sure He could. God can do anything. But that's not the point.

God is more committed to growing us into His image than having us sit back and comfortably sail through life like babies feeding on a bottle and being cared for. He is preparing us for future ruling and reigning with Jesus. This requires us to actively participate in the process. A baby doesn't learn to walk by sitting and never getting up. He walks by getting up and taking steps, falling down, and then getting back up again. Persistence and pursuit of the goal results in walking!

> **God is more committed to growing us into His image than having us sit back and comfortably sail through life.**

Anything worthwhile takes pursuit and action. Ask any gold medalist, concert pianist, or parent. Likewise, finding truth—Jesus, who is the truth—will necessitate our pursuit. I encourage you to seek truth with all your heart, because God promises in Jeremiah 29:13 that if you seek Him with your whole heart, you will find Him.

> **Anything worthwhile takes pursuit and action. Ask any gold medalist, concert pianist, or parent.**

Faith: A Critical Ingredient

I wish I could testify that pursuit in and of itself is all we need to successfully navigate this trek that God has us on, but there is another critical ingredient. Hints of this element are interspersed subtly within my stories. That element is faith—that quality that can move mountains! "If you have faith as small as a mustard seed, you can say to this mountain, 'Move from here to there,' and it will move" (Matthew 17:20 NIV).

Having faith is easier said than done, yet it is critical. I'm not sure which comes first, pursuit or faith, but it might not matter. Without both in the mix, our journey will stall.

Years ago, one of my sons asked me what faith was and how to get it. At the time, I felt I failed him miserably since the concept was difficult for me to explain. Simplistically, I think faith is believing that God is who He says He is and can do what He says He can do. As we step out believing this and putting it to the test in our lives, God shows Himself faithful.

When I first came to the Lord, I knew nothing about having faith, but I heard the gospel of truth and simply believed it. After that, I began to learn what God said about Himself, including His character, His ways, His promises, and His mission.

The more I pursued truth and knowledge of Him, the more I stepped out and trusted His Word and believed it. He was always faithful to me. It is who He is!

Remember when God took me to John 8:32: "You will know the truth, and the truth will set you free"? These words contain a promise that required action on my part. Not only did I have to pursue truth, but I also had to believe that what God said was true. Truth—His truth—would set me free.

As I agreed with God's Word, I was exercising faith. I was believing in something that God said was true but wasn't yet a reality in my life. This is exactly how the author of Hebrews defines faith: "Faith is confidence in what we hope for and assurance about what we do not see" (Hebrews 11:1 NIV). God partners with us through our faith to perform His purpose. It's not that He can't do things without our faith, but God is blessed by our faith. Finish reading Hebrews 11, and you will see. God commends those who believe Him in faith.

Faith, however, isn't blind. It is simply choosing to believe what God says even when, at the moment, you can't see it.

When these Christian leaders before us longed for and needed God to move in their lives, God called them to a life of faith. He calls us to this life of faith too (Romans 1:17). Some people contend that faith makes no sense. There may be some truth in that, and I guess maybe it has something to do with the phrase "blind faith." Faith, however, isn't blind. Having faith is simply choosing to believe what God says, even when, at the moment, you can't see it.

Solomon also explains this process of faith in the book of Proverbs when he encourages us to "trust in the Lord with all your heart, and do not lean on your own understanding. In all your ways acknowledge him, and he will make straight your paths" (Proverbs 3:5–6). God promises that if we trust in Him and have faith in Him and not in ourselves, He will make the path straight that we are traveling on.

I personally experienced something similar to this. I chose to take God at His Word and not lean on my own understanding of my broken heart. While I was pursuing truth, freedom was produced in my life. As we stretch our faith and believe that God is able, we will find Him faithful and capable.

The Spirit of Truth

Several times while our family was traveling in the Mediterranean, Italy, and Israel, we decided to take a guided tour to learn more about our destinations. The guides were very knowledgeable and taught us a great deal that we would never have known otherwise.

In His overwhelming love, God understood that in order to reach our destination of knowing Him and making Him known here on earth as His image bearers, we would need a guide to enlighten us and show us the way. As Jesus walked the earth prior to His crucifixion, He served as a guide, leading many people into the truth. However, He made it clear that because He was a man, He was limited in His ability to touch all. Therefore, it was to the believer's advantage that He would leave the earth. He left but not before promising that His Father would not leave them alone but would send them another guide who would instead dwell within them and would lead them into all truth (John 16:7, 13). This guide is the third person of the Trinity—the Holy Spirit.

Throughout the Old and New Testaments, from Genesis to Revelation, we see the presence of the Holy Spirit. In the Old Testament, His impact was generally from outside as He influenced those He touched. However, Christ's death and resurrection made the way for the Holy Spirit to dwell within us (1 Corinthians 3:16). When we give our hearts to Christ, we are encouraged to receive this precious gift—the gift of the Holy Spirit.

Many people think this gift, provided by God to guide us through life successfully, is an amorphous entity. However, the Bible clearly teaches that the Holy Spirit is a separate being with feelings, abilities, and roles that are distinct from God the Father and God the Son (Isaiah 63:10; Matthew 12:31; Acts 7:51; Galatians 5:22–23; Ephesians 4:30; Hebrews 10:29). Although it is not my purpose to give an exhaustive exposé on the person of the Holy Spirit, a general understanding of His role and purpose in our lives is essential if we hope to reconnect with God's original design and purpose. Next is an incomplete yet helpful list of the varied and key roles the Holy Spirit plays in our lives.

Roles of the Holy Spirit

- Helps us .... Romans 8:26
- Guides us .... John 16:13
- Teaches us .... John 14:26
- Speaks to us .... Revelation 2:7
- Reveals to us .... 1 Corinthians 2:10
- Instructs us.. Acts 8:29
- Testifies of Jesus... John 15:26
- Comforts us .... Acts 9:31
- Fills us .... Acts 4:31
- Strengthens us... Ephesians 3:16
- Convicts us of sin... John 16:8
- Prays for us .... Romans 8:26
- Renews us .... Titus 3:5
- Transforms us .... 2 Corinthians 3:18
- Leads us .... Romans 8:14
- Sanctifies us.. 2 Thessalonians 2:13
- Seals us .... Ephesians 1:13
- Delivers us.. Psalm 34:17
- Pursues us .... John 6:44
- Calls us... Acts 13:2
- Bears witness to truth .... Romans 9:1
- Brings His fruit... Galatians 5:22–23
- Lives in us.. 1 Corinthians 3:16
- Frees us .... Romans 8:2
- Gives us wisdom.. James 1:5
- Gives gifts .... 1 Corinthians 12:1–11

I am struck by the many ways the Holy Spirit has impacted my life. Some I was aware of at the time, but many I wasn't. One particular role jumps out at me: *Pursues!* What? I didn't

Before I even knew about God, He was pursuing me.

realize that decades ago as a young nursing student, I was being pursued by the Holy Spirit. Even before I knew about God, He was pursuing me.

Peter Scazzero's words highlight this truth: "Christianity is not about our disciplined pursuit of God, but about God's relentless pursuit of us— to the point of dying on a cross for us that we might become His friends."[10]

With embarrassment, I have to admit I always thought I pursued God first. Is that my ignorance or my pride? Either way, I can remember my surprise when I learned that the Holy Spirit is the pursuer from first to last. This doesn't excuse us from our need to pursue, but the fact remains that our relationship and the subsequent journey to destiny is initiated by Him.

Many times during the past forty-plus years since I first gave my heart to Jesus in a little college campus chapel, I have allowed busyness or frustration to cause me to drift away from the Lord. For years, I thought it was my longing for the lost closeness with the Lord that drove me back to His presence. However, my desire to return to closeness with God was actually initiated by the Holy Spirit pursuing me, wooing me back to intimacy with God. Shock of shocks! It's not all about me—it's about Him!

I could write an entire book about how the Holy Spirit permeated my life. One particular time, I felt the Holy Spirit not only speak truth, but also provide comfort, give hope, and strengthen me. I was in the early days of facing the truth of my heart, and I was filled with overwhelming fear—fear of people, fear of my emotions, fear that I would never change, and fear that my kids would be irreparably damaged by me. You know—fear. I remember at the time calling out to God in my torment.

I was reading in the Bible, and I came to Psalm 34:4: "I sought the Lord, and he answered me and delivered me from *all* my fears" (emphasis mine). The words seemed to jump off the page, and I seized them. I was so thankful that the Holy Spirit led me to these words.

They became God's promises to me and were life-giving assurances that I wouldn't always be riddled with and bound by fear.

There is a deep fear that has hounded me since I was quite young. God is faithfully delivering me from this fear, but I recall a memory that demonstrated that it was a full-blown paralyzing fear.

My fear of snakes began as a youngster, probably even before I can recall. My earliest memory of this fear is as a preschooler when I would not even touch a book that I knew had a picture of a snake in it. Through the years, the fear became deeply rooted, and I avoided snakes in all forms, even in books, in pictures, or at the zoo.

One year, after visiting my mom on Martha's Vineyard, my husband and I took our kids to the Boston Children's Museum. We were having a wonderful time interacting and showing our kids all the exhibits. We walked into a little room, and right in front of us was a cage with a huge snake in it. I was filled with so much terror that I couldn't move. I just stood there with no escape in sight. Looking ahead at my husband, I silently beseeched him to come back and get me; I was completely stuck.

All of a sudden, the words "he who is in you is greater than he who is in the world" (1 John 4:4) quietly entered my mind. I heard them but was still immobilized. The words kept replaying in my mind, and finally I mentally gripped them and willingly repeated them over and over. Slowly, my legs began to move and propel me out of the room. Shaking, I gave thanks to the Holy Spirit for His ability to free and deliver me.

Having been supplied by God with the most important and beneficial gift I will ever need, I rely on the Holy Spirit daily. I haven't always recognized His role and input in my life. Nevertheless, He has faithfully provided what I need in the moment as I continue along God's path toward wholeness and discover the truth of who I was, who God made me to be in Christ, and what His purpose is for my life. Trekking through the various terrains of life, I'm grateful for the Holy Spirit's tangible presence and activities on my behalf—making the path straight.

However, I am continually cognizant that He is not going to drag me passively through life. I have to partner with Him by pursuing truth and mixing it with faith.

The "Why" of It

When I think of "pursuing" something, there are many other words that come to mind, such as hunt, quest, track down, and search. These words definitely didn't describe me in my younger years, and quite frankly, I can remember a time when this whole concept of pursuit drove me crazy.

My husband, who at the time was my boyfriend, used to ask questions and wonder about things all the time: "I wonder how that works." "Why do you think they are doing things that way?" "I wonder what that means." He was always looking into the "whys" of things and searching for understanding and wisdom.

I often thought to myself, *Who cares?* However, I have come to find this trait endearing and incredibly useful. Why? Because John knows everything! At least we joke about that together. Actually, I have learned a lot from my husband. He is a natural researcher and a true scholar. His inquisitive nature has filled him with a breadth of knowledge and wisdom that I now feel privileged to be a part of.

My sister, Melanie, also has this inquisitive mind. She is forever posing insightful questions that delve deep and serve to uncover the heart of a matter. Both people have been great tutors to me, benefiting me as I probe and search out truth with questions.

As I excavate the issues of my heart, two of the most useful questions I have learned to ask God are *Why do I feel this way, Lord?* and *Why do I behave this way?* As I have asked these questions, God has faithfully answered them through His still, small voice, His Word, a picture or vision, journaling, or a random thought that pops into my head.

A dear friend once said that it wasn't important to know why, for all we need is Jesus. I do agree that Jesus is everything we need and that He is the truth, but I contend that the "why" is a method Jesus uses to unearth the faulty foundations and mindsets planted over the years so that His truth can be replanted.

The "why" is a method Jesus uses to unearth the faulty foundations and mindsets planted over the years so that His truth can be replanted.

I was born prematurely—six weeks early, to be exact. I weighed only four pounds, and I needed to remain in an enclosed isolette for the first month of my life.

Decades later, I was talking to the Lord about how I had this odd sense that no matter what I did, I felt a separation between me and other people. This feeling had nagged at me for years. Finally, I asked the Lord why I felt that way. What was it related to? As I sat quietly, I immediately saw a picture of a baby in an isolette. With that picture came the realization that the baby was me, and that I had been separated from people. It made total sense to me; the memory was still alive.

When the Lord answers your questions, you never want to leave it at just the discovery. Not only do you need to expose the issue, but then you need to deal with it in light of God's truth. In subsequent chapters, we will specifically examine how to deal with these issues more extensively. For now, let me share how I handled the picture the Lord gave me. I asked another question: *Lord, where were You while I was lying in that isolette?*

The picture that came to me caused me to burst out laughing. Jesus has an incredible sense of humor. I saw that same isolette, but this time Jesus was crammed into that tiny little space with me. Of course, I don't think Jesus was actually crammed in there with me, but the message was clear: He was with me, and I was not alone. Bringing laughter to my heart with that vision forever dispelled the effect of the memory and my nagging sense of separation from people.

The asking of questions that day brought truth to my heart and left freedom in its wake.

Asking questions that day brought truth to my heart and freedom to my soul. If you have never experienced the power of asking God questions, I would encourage you to begin. The Bible is filled with examples of many individuals doing the same. As we desire and pursue the truth, both the truth of our hearts and God's truth, He will be faithful to supply it.

Mining for Truth

When I think of pursuing something, the word "mining" often comes to mind. Pursuit gives the idea of chasing, tracking, and searching, but mining takes pursuit deeper. I love *Merriam-Webster*'s definition of "mining": "To dig under to gain access or cause the collapse of (an enemy position)."[11]

"To dig under to gain access or cause the collapse of." That is interesting (more on the enemy piece later). This definition begs the question, "What are we digging under to gain access to or to cause to collapse?" I see the answer as twofold in our pursuit of truth. We are digging into our "truths" whether they are right or wrong, and then we are collapsing the ones not in agreement with God's truth. We are also extracting God's truth in order to supplant the faulty "truth" we believe.

In chapter two, I revealed some of the ways my faulty foundation had established a mindset contrary to the truth. These things became entrenched and had to be "mined" out and replaced with the truth of what God says. There is a verse that talks about this process: "We demolish arguments and every pretension that sets itself up against the knowledge of God, and we take captive every thought to make it obedient to Christ" (2 Corinthians 10:5 NIV).

When I began counseling, this was the process God launched me into. He knew I was filled with false arguments and thoughts contrary to His purpose of founding me on a basis of truth and love. Therefore, He had to "mine" these things out of my heart so that the truth could be received and planted.

I have hinted at an important detail that needs to be highlighted: God "mines" as we partner with Him. When I was new in this mining process, I wanted to get it over with as quickly as possible. At the time, I didn't understand that this is a lifelong pursuit, and I told God to dig it all up and confront me with all the "junk."

How little I knew about the Holy Spirit! He was gentle, kind, and loving as He explained that it would be cruel (and would possibly destroy me) to have me face all of the trauma and abuse at one time. Thus, He taught me to trust His leading and not to be a bull in a china shop or to dig madly to excavate everything in sight. I needed to let God run the excavator. I needed to trust His timing to allow things to bubble to the surface when I needed to address them.

I had no prior concept of archeological digging. This was an exercise in trusting God and His purpose, knowing that He was a masterful archeologist who promised to transform me as I submitted to His gentle, cautious, and deliberate digging.

Mining is not just for the bad things in life ... but it is also to expose the good.

Over the years, and contrary to my original thinking, I have learned that mining is not just for the bad things in life, such as examining the abuse, traumas, and wrong thinking we have, but it is also to expose the good. As archeologists excavate, they discover many things that are useless junk. What keeps them going, though, is the drive to find the treasures.

Admittedly, it was difficult for me to imagine finding anything that I would treasure, but as God emptied me of that which was painful, there was room left for me to see the treasures that were buried amid the rubble. Being able to have clearer vision developed a heart of thankfulness in me.

For example, I more easily see my parents through undistorted lenses. Where I once saw only the bad, I now also see the good. Thankfully, before my mom died last year, I was able to talk with her and thank her for some of the good things she gave to me. As damaged as her heart was, I am so grateful that she never wavered in her love, support, and devotion to me and my beloved siblings. She also taught me to passionately pursue healing, my interests, creativity, and valuing others. I'm thankful my perspective has changed.

Recently, while vacationing on Martha's Vineyard, almost every place I went held memories for me. Instead of hating the Vineyard as I had done for years (unbeknownst to me, it represented my painful background), my heart was fully open to the island, and I appreciated the safe haven and wonderful memories it held for me. These treasures, and many others, have been the gifts God helped me mine, ridding me of the unpleasant debris and exposing the gems.

As Christians, we know that the truth is found in the Bible, and we are encouraged to read the Word daily. This practice is critical to health and uprooting faulty mindsets.

There are so many ways we can mine and ingest the truth of the Word. I have used many ways, including listening to the Word, teachings, and podcasts; watching videos; and reading Christian books. However, I can't say enough about inductive Bible studies. That's where I learned to study and dig treasures out of the Word for myself. It was through these studies that God used His Word to teach, heal, reveal, convict, and lead me. I heartily endorse them and encourage you to try one.

Unfortunately, in our world of instant gratification, we have been lulled into thinking that easy and quick is always the best way. That certainly is not true. Mining for truth and excavating for treasures takes diligent, thoughtful exploration. Inductive Bible studies can nurture you in your pursuit.

One last practical technique in mining for truth, whether exploring your background or pursuing intimacy with God, is journaling. I know that many people say, "I hate journaling," "I don't have time for journaling," or even "What's journaling got to do with it?" I understand. I've probably said those same words at one time or another. However, years ago a friend taught me about red-letter journaling. This technique helped me learn to hear God's voice better, to obtain His truth, and to keep a record of things God shared with me over the years. You might try it and find it to be a valuable tool.

Essentially, while I am reading my Bible in prayer, I write out questions, concerns, feelings, or thoughts in my journal with a blue or black pen. After I finish writing, I sit quietly and wait for God to respond. When I sense Him speaking or sharing a passage of Scripture, I start writing it in my journal with a red, or different color, pen. I continue writing until I sense God is done. If God has led me to a Scripture passage, I write it down, along with my impressions of what He is saying to me through those Bible verses.

When my friend first shared this technique that she had learned from her Youth With A Mission (YWAM) instructor, I was a bit doubtful. What if what I wrote in red wasn't from God, or what if it was coming from me, or worse yet, from the Enemy? Maybe I would be led astray.

I turned to prayer and asked God what He thought about it. I felt impressed by God to critically evaluate any journaling in the same way that I would evaluate any teaching or sermons. Was it consistent with His character, His ways, His mission, and Scripture? If it was, then I could feel fairly confident it was from God. However, He encouraged me to share it with a trusted believer who could also test it. To give you an idea of what I mean, I will provide an example from my journal. (In my journal, my question is in black and the response is in red.)

Lord, what are qualities You placed in me that You like?

> I love your gaiety and excitement. I love how you're full of energy and get so excited when talking to others. I love your sensitivity and your heart for others. You long for justice and what is right and fair. You don't want anyone to be oppressed or hurting. I love how you encourage people to be all they can be, or if they are struggling, then you come alongside to encourage them. I like your childlikeness. I love how you want people to see and understand Me so they can grow closer to Me and be all they are destined to be. I love how you like things in order and how you try to bring order into places that are unorganized and scattered.

Believe that God is who He says He is and will do in your life what He says He will.

In your journey toward being God's image bearer, and while discovering His original purpose for you, I want to encourage you to pursue truth as you exercise faith. Believe that God is who He says He is and will do in your life what He says He will do and is in the process of doing. He will lead you using the power and working of the Holy Spirit. The Holy Spirit will assist you in exposing your "truth," whether it is faulty and in need of replacing, or whether it is in line with His truth and should be treasured.

May you receive the Holy Spirit as He faithfully takes you on this journey. If you have not received Him, if you desire to grow in your relationship with Him, or if you desire to "be filled with the Spirit" (Ephesians 5:18), below is a simple prayer you can pray.

Prayer for Infilling of the Holy Spirit

Father God, I thank You that You have given the Holy Spirit as a gift to help me grow in truth and intimacy and to fulfill the purpose You have for me. I pray that You would baptize me in the Holy Spirit and fill me to overflowing with Him. Teach me, God, to know Him more, allowing Him to fully work and be manifested in and through me. Thank You, God, for Your Spirit.

Exposing Areas of Captivity

*What comes out of a person is what defiles him.
For from within, out of the heart of man, come
evil thoughts, sexual immorality, theft, murder,
adultery, coveting, wickedness, deceit, sensuality,
envy, slander, pride, foolishness. All these evil things
come from within, and they defile a person.*
Mark 7:20-23

I want to warn you that we are diving into murky waters. This will not always be fun to read, but it is necessary. If what you read triggers challenging issues of your own, please know that it is okay to put the book down, breathe, and take a break. I wish we were sitting in comfy chairs, with coffee in hand and a crackling fire lending its warmth as we share such things and then pray together. If at this point, or any other, a more personal conversation would be helpful, please seek out a trusted friend or counselor you might confide in. For now, let's pray before we begin:

> Father God, I pray right now in the name of Jesus that You would be with us as we continue to dialogue about challenging heart issues. Surround us with Your loving presence, lead us into truth, and bring healing to all who are in need. Thank You that You never leave or forsake us and that You

are the One who leads us on toward wholeness and the purpose You have prepared us for from the beginning. Protect us from the Evil One, who desires to thwart Your plan for our lives. Lead us in the way everlasting, bringing us beside the still waters where You restore our souls. In Jesus's name, Amen.

Sooner or later, our travel along life's journey toward purpose will take us back to the beginning, where we will come face to face with our background baggage and entrenched mindsets. While we are there, we cannot escape the sad reality that much of what we experienced, along with our ensuing mindsets, developed as the result of harm by someone else. Essentially, we suffered an injustice and unmerited harm.

Many times, these injustices were unintentionally inflicted, but sometimes they were intentional. I experienced injustices that were unintentionally inflicted by my parents. Whether unintentional or not, their actions resulted in personal injurious consequences.

On the flip side, the sexual abuse I endured was intentionally perpetrated. The abuser purposely mistreated me for his pleasure. Whether unintentional or intentional, all injustices we suffer, both big and small, result in harm and injury to our personal development.

When you are trying to understand injustices, it is important for you to remember that God never intended for mankind to suffer them. As I mentioned in an earlier chapter, God designed each of us to grow and develop in an atmosphere of love and absolute truth. Any time we didn't, in His eyes an injustice occurred.[12]

Make no mistake, God is grieved by the injustices we've experienced. They were never His plan for us.

Make no mistake—God is grieved by the injustices we've experienced. They were never His plan for us.

According to Brian Brennt and Mike Riches, "It is common for individuals to suffer from an injustice and never recognize it. The injustice has become so much a part of life, that it seems normal."[13] This point was exactly what I mentioned earlier about children normalizing trauma and hurtful situations. It becomes so much a part of their story that it represents normality. However, the challenge comes when the injustice suffered is minimized.

I'll never forget when I first started realizing the enormity of the injustices I had experienced as a child, for I had normalized them for decades. I became upset with God. Where was He when my relative sexually abused me or when we were placed in that crazy therapy? Thankfully, God was as unaffected by my anger as He was by David's in the Bible.

As I was fussing and questioning Him, I heard His gentle, calm voice say, "It was not My will for you, but I provided your defense mechanisms to protect your soul until you knew Me and received My healing."

It wasn't the answer I expected, but somehow it calmed me. It was comforting to know that God had been with me and was protecting me, even to the point of enabling me to normalize the abuse I suffered, which allowed me to continue functioning. From the start, God's intention was to heal and restore.

There comes a point when this ability to normalize is no longer beneficial to our soul, and ignoring past injustices "does nothing but harm us further."[14] To grow deeper in the truth and in intimacy with God so we accurately reflect God's image, it is imperative for us to face past injustices. You might ask, "Why?"

The answer lies in what is produced by avoided and undealt-with injustices: strongholds! Considering that injustices create a vacuum of love and truth in our lives, "Any relationship or situation in our lives that does not reflect the full truth or love of God is an opportunity for the enemy to build strongholds."[15] The development of these strongholds on the hotbed of injustices is what places us in captivity and prohibits us from walking in the fullness of Christ and our purpose in Him.

Strongholds of the Enemy

When I think of strongholds, I am transported to military-type movies I've seen or to the countless forts I've visited over the years. It is difficult at times to grasp the militaristic vocabulary used in the Bible. We might think it applies only to biblical times and that it is not applicable to us in this modern age. Yes, we've seen recent wars, but unless we've been directly involved, they seem distant and unreal to us. However, I'm sure that for anyone who has been deployed to Afghanistan or has had a loved one involved, war was real to them and was not just what movies and books are made of.

Unfortunately, even if you are unaware of it, you are currently on active duty in a divine war. We have established that God has an enemy—Satan—and by default, Christians do too. If you didn't realize this and if this is a scary concept for you, let me assure you that the book of Revelation clearly affirms that God (and His church) are victorious in the end.

For years, this reality of being in a war with Satan and his minions terrified me. I didn't fully understand that the final victory had been secured. Sadly, I didn't know God well enough to comprehend that He is the Creator and that nothing can stand against Him.

Satan is jealous of God's love for us, and therefore he hates us.

Satan does know this, but it doesn't stop him from trying to take mankind captive, hurting God's heart in the process. Satan is jealous of God's love for us, and therefore he hates us. His strategy, then, is to deceive mankind and turn them away from God and His Word. He was successful in this with Adam and Eve, and he has continued to use this strategy in battle ever since.

His aim has never changed. He "is aggressively seeking to destroy you, render your life useless, and rob you of your rightful inheritance in Christ."[16]

We don't always like to think about it, but the Bible corroborates this truth in 1 Peter 5:8: "Your adversary the devil prowls around like a roaring lion, seeking someone to devour." Satan is after your faith, your relationship with God, and your destiny in Christ.

Accepting that we have an enemy who is doing everything he can to destroy us through the creation of strongholds in our lives, it is important for us to understand what a stronghold is. Interestingly, *Merriam-Webster* defines it as "a place dominated by a particular group or marked by a particular characteristic."[17] This describes exactly what the Union Army attempted to achieve over the Confederate army, and vice versa, during the Civil War. Each tried to take dominion over as much land as they could. Our enemy is no different.

In the *Freedom Class Manual,* authors Brennt and Riches further illuminate the meaning by bringing clarity to the military analogy, allowing us to gain greater understanding as it specifically relates to us:

> In a literal physical sense, a stronghold serves as a military camp, a fortified defense (for a territory), a base of operations, or a headquarters. A spiritual stronghold works in a very similar way to a material one. A stronghold is made up of sin expressed in a person's thoughts, beliefs, attitudes, philosophies, actions, and values that oppose the truth of God. Strongholds are a "launching pad" for enemy influence in our lives.[18]

The key principle is that the Enemy takes territory in your heart as a result of sin, either your own sin or that imposed by injustice. This territory becomes

The Enemy takes territory in your heart as a result of sin, either yours or that imposed by injustice.

the "base of operations" from which the Enemy tries to hold you captive and negatively influence you. No matter what the cause of the sin is that you experience, the door of your heart has been opened, and the Enemy has gladly taken dominion over this territory.

Let me give an example to further illustrate this concept. When I was a toddler, I was sexually abused by a family member. The injustice I experienced at the hands of this man engendered intense fear. Consequently, his sin made room for the Enemy to influence me and take territory of my heart by pushing the fear of men deep into my soul. Subsequently, I began to fear not just my abuser, but all men.

By the time I was about ten years old, I was so afraid of men that when my friend and I were in her parents' room, I couldn't even go near the father's side of the bed! That friend's father hadn't done anything to harm me, but the fear in my heart had developed into a stronghold that encompassed all men.

The fear continued and proliferated throughout my life, engendering fearfulness about almost everything. It was something I had no control over. I was completely at its mercy. It rendered me captive and placed me under the Enemy's influence.

Have you ever felt completely out of control regarding something you feel? You try over and over to conquer it—with no success. My friend Randy Young defines strongholds as "anything contrary to the Word and will of God in our lives that we feel powerless to do anything about."[19] A stronghold is anything that we feel powerless to do anything about or unable to change. That describes exactly how I felt about my fears. Can you identify with Randy's definition? If so, you might be dealing with a stronghold. If this is the case, you are not fighting yourself, but you are fighting a very real enemy whose intent is to destroy you.

The good news? Jesus Christ made the way to freedom from all strongholds.

The good news is that Jesus Christ made the way to freedom from all strongholds. The Word of God promises us that there is no weapon or plan the Enemy uses in our lives that will prosper (Isaiah 54:17).

After thirty years of walking with the Lord and allowing Him to cleanse me from strongholds, I can confirm that His Word is true; I am living proof! Thankfully, Jesus did the work for our freedom when He died on the cross. As believers, however, we are called to actuate what He has already accomplished by standing on the truth and using the authority Christ gave us. We have to do the battle.

Sometimes our battles are easily won, but other times the Enemy is deeply entrenched and the battle takes longer and requires more persistence. My stronghold of fear is a perfect example of a hard-won battle that required prolonged engagement. I have learned that the Enemy never plays fair. One weapon he uses against us is discouragement because he wants us to think that things will never change.

If you feel Satan barraging you with assaults, I want to tell you the words a dear friend spoke over me while on her deathbed: "The Lord told me you are safe!" I am deeply grateful for those divine words of assurance. They are no less true for you. You are safe in the arms of Jesus!

Isaiah assures us of our safety.

"So shall they fear the name of the Lord from the west, and His glory from the rising of the sun; when the enemy comes in like a flood, the Spirit of the Lord will lift up a standard against him" (Isaiah 59:19 NKJV).

Bound by Lies

We are safe. However, there are many ways the Enemy seeks to gain access to our hearts through established strongholds, all of them having to do with sin. It could be our own sin, or it could be externally inflicted injustice.

It seems unfair that strongholds are created by injustices since first we had to endure them, and then we have to deal with the repercussions due to the strongholds formed in our heart. It isn't fair, but you've probably already figured out by now that life isn't always fair.

In order for us to uproot strongholds, it is critical for us to understand how a stronghold is created. When an injustice has occurred, we internalize messages as a consequence. These messages may be true, although more often than not they are false and are often subconsciously constructed. Once the lie is internalized, the perpetual agreement with it or belief of it fortifies the Enemy's influence and effectively creates a stronghold. Look at the following personal examples:

- Injustice incurred: sexual abuse by a male family member. He added fear by threatening that the police would take me away from my family if I ever told what happened. To top it off, I was told by my abuser that I was worthless and should be ashamed of myself!

Internalized lies that developed as a result of the injustice:
  - You are worthless and are no better than trash.
  - You should be ashamed of your behavior.
  - Men are scary and only want one thing.
  - Police are to be feared because they take people away from their families.
  - Intimacy with men is bad.
  - Don't speak truth.

Strongholds created in my life: fear, self-hatred, shame, and guilt.

- Injustice incurred: sexual abuse and the perverted "therapy" endured as a child.

Internalized lies that developed as a result of the experience:
  - I must suffer in silence.
  - I am powerless and can't say anything.

- I can't say no to anything and must go along with what people want me to do.
- Strongholds created in my life: I am a victim.

All injustices, big or small, have the same potential of building strongholds.

As you look at the injustices I suffered, it might be easy for you to minimize your own experience of injustices if they don't seem as bad. However, it is important to remember that all injustices, big or small, have the same potential of building strongholds. It is very detrimental to disqualify an injustice because it didn't measure up to someone else's. Doing so robs you of the opportunity for healing.

There are several things that are helpful to understand about lies. First, we generally don't consciously know they are lies, or we don't realize that we believe them. Often, the lies have become so embedded in our belief system that we see them as normal. The lies I mentioned above were so ingrained in my soul that I had no idea they were present, let alone that they were lies. They became truth to me.

That's the absurd thing about lies—we often think they are the truth. The Enemy intends it this way. However, just because we believe something is true doesn't mean it is. The Enemy neatly disguises lies so that we receive them as truth. Sadly, I discovered I was filled with lies that infected all areas of my life.

Once a lie is implanted by the Enemy through an injustice (if it is not rapidly contradicted by truth), it is often embraced and agreed with. Once agreed with, the Enemy continues to bring situations into our lives that will reinforce the lie, leading us to agree with it again and again. As we "accept the lies, meditating on them and rehearsing them over and over, our mental torment increases,"[20] and they become more entrenched and part of our belief structure. This unholy stronghold then infects our lives.

I remember once as a child feeling sick and sitting outside my mother's bedroom at night needing her, yet not being able to call out. I was too scared. I lay next to her door, quietly crying until finally I fell asleep.

Why? I had internalized the lies: I must suffer in silence; I am a powerless victim and am ashamed of myself; I would be a bad girl to wake her. My mom would have been horrified if she had known why I was lying on the floor outside her room all night.

Stepping back, I can see how silly and sad this was, but as a child, these lies were my deeply implanted truth. They affected even the small situations in my life.

Believing in the lies affects who we become as individuals and interferes with who God has designed us to be. "Once you believe what is false, what you hear, see, or do is filtered through the lens of that false belief."[21] The lies believed become our value system, which in turn affects how we behave and affects the choices we make in life. The false beliefs pervert understanding of our identity, value, and purpose as well as our view of God's identity.

> **Believing in the lies affects who we become as individuals and interferes with who God has designed us to be.**

Growing up with so many false beliefs about my identity, I found it difficult to receive the truth about who God said I was. In my mind, I was worthless and ugly, so how could I ever embrace the truth of being a saint who was loved and seated in heavenly realms with Christ? How could I ever believe that God had a design and purpose for me? It was unfathomable. I was nothing. It is horrible to endure injustices, but to live with these aftereffects is brutal.

Thankfully, God knows all about our lives—the lies, the truth, and everything in between. His desire is to "proclaim liberty to the captives, and the opening of the prison to those who are bound" (Isaiah 61:1). In His wisdom, He knows how to expose the lies in our hearts and how to securely plant our feet on His truth.

I had believed many falsehoods. I now know that God found each one grievous. He was grieving that my life had been shaped by lies and enemy-inflicted pain that prohibited me from experiencing the abundant life He had intended. God is grieved for you as well, and He wants to uproot anything in your life that is contrary to His truth so that your feet are firmly planted on Him and you can experience the life He has planned for you.

Memories Are Powerful

Memories of our past are powerful things that are used consciously and subconsciously to inform our past, present, and future. They are the subject of much research and scholarly consideration.

Being a pastor and not a trained psychologist or psychiatrist, I readily admit I have limited knowledge when it comes to the breadth of wisdom available about memories and triggers. My knowledge is from personal and ministerial experiences and reading resources as well as from the Bible. However, there is a plethora of resources and information available (some of which I have included in the Resource List) as well as many qualified professional Christian counselors ready and willing to assist.

When I first went to counseling, I thought I had to remember everything that ever happened to me in order to receive healing from God. I was determined, no matter how painful it would be, to force the memories into consciousness. It was an impossible task for sure, but I desperately wanted complete healing and wholeness no matter the cost.

Since that time, I have realized that remembering isn't always critical for healing. I have personally received healing of wounds and deliverance from strongholds despite my deficit of memories. Certainly there were plenty of things I remembered, but I had little recall about much of my childhood—both the good and the not so good.

There is increasing research about the challenges of memories because of how they are stored and accessed as well as the effect that memories have on individuals. As mentioned in the book *Trauma-Informed Care*, "Memories of trauma are stored in the brain differently than non-traumatic memories."[22] The memories themselves are often not accessible, and therefore they are difficult to convey verbally.

I have certainly found this to be true, as my memories of the abuse I suffered are minimal. This may in part be the result of having been abused at such a young age when my language and thought processing was in its formative stage. What I do remember is fragmented and is more of an impression. These vague memories are challenging to decipher since they are often unclear or obscure. I have discovered that it is important to be aware that memories aren't always trustworthy; some can be clear, but others might be patchy and disjointed.

This point is highlighted by Dr. Dan B. Allender, who explains that memories in and of themselves can often be unclear, incomplete, and/or misconstrued. He contends that this does not mean we should discount any memories, but rather we should use them, in whatever form, as a means of providing important information that enlightens us about our present.[23]

Either way, whether clear or fragmented, memories offer us insight into our background. With the guidance of the Holy Spirit, we can receive valuable information that helps us extract both injustices and positive influences in our backgrounds.

For example, one thing I value in myself is my creativity. I attribute this quality to the influence of my parents. Why? Because I have so many memories of them not only being creative in their work, but also doing things with me when I was a child. I'll never forget making Valentine's Day cards for my classmates and being so proud of the cards. I can also warmly recall sewing my own clothes, needlepointing Christmas gifts for my family, and knitting a sweater for my mom. These are memories I cherish because of their positive impact on me, and subsequently, because they provided the motivation for me to replicate these memories with my kids.

On the other hand, as Dr. Allender described, there are memories I would swear by, while other people's memory of the same events might differ from mine. For instance, I could swear that my mom and dad physically fought a lot. I remember watching and being very scared and upset. However, my mom contends it only happened once. Whether her memory or mine is right isn't the point. What is important to explore is how the experience affected me then and how it affects me now.

The event effectively painted a picture of how conflict was handled, and it ultimately underscored for me that conflict was scary and should be avoided. The Enemy used this traumatic memory, and others, to reinforce lies about conflict that I unknowingly carried through childhood and into my adulthood. Exploring the memory and its effect when I was an adult served as a touch point that exposed my faulty beliefs about conflict.

In no way do I want to diminish the power of memories and how their reality influences our everyday lives. Too many people have been wounded by counselors or friends who didn't believe that their traumatic memories were factual. My point is simply to highlight that memories are real, and whether complete or fragmented, they represent experiences and provide clues to the belief structures we hold.

Trusting the Holy Spirit to disclose insights from your memories will be beneficial in uncovering lie structures the Enemy built as a consequence of injustices. Better yet, it will enable the Holy Spirit to heal wounds and tear down strongholds.

A Case for Triggers

As mentioned, memories give valuable insight as we make our way down the path to healing. However, they are not the only means of acquiring a roadmap of the false belief systems that we developed throughout our lives. Triggers also supply indispensable information as we allow God to expose them.

Triggers are "those events or situations which in some way resemble or symbolize a past trauma to individual survivors. These triggers cause the body to return to the 'fight, flight, or freeze' reaction common to traumatic situations."[24]

Do you remember my experience at the children's museum when I froze at the sight of the snake? This was a trigger. Similarly, another time I was window shopping in London with my mom, and I unexpectedly walked by a person who had a large snake wrapped around him. Without even thinking, I took off and ran around the corner with little thought to my mother's welfare. This was the same trigger in a different situation: freeze—flight. These triggers pointed to a childhood trauma of which I had no memory.

When explored under the influence of the Holy Spirit, our triggers can help us connect with the emotions we had as children but that went unexpressed. I have found this to be beneficial when unearthing the faulty beliefs formed during my childhood.

For example, I had two self-involved parents who pursued their own interests while leaving me alone a lot. As a result, I had no platform from which to express my feelings or the messages I internalized. However, after I married John, and his duties at the hospital consistently required him to be away (leaving me alone again), all of my unexpressed feelings came hurtling toward him. Talk about fight! The poor guy would call me to tell me he was delayed, and I would let him have it.

Triggers generally work like this: your emotions escalate from zero to one hundred in a matter of seconds. Poor John! He had no idea that the message I wrongly perceived about his delay was connected all the way back to my parents. I felt left alone. I felt as if he didn't want to be with me. I felt as if I wasn't valuable. I felt as if everything else was more important to John than me and the kids. In reality, none of these things were true. They were childhood messages and festering wounds that had not yet been dealt with.

Thankfully, as I learned about triggers and how to allow God to trace them back to their source, I was healed and freed from the underlying painful issues from which they stemmed. Once God healed my heart, I could respond to circumstances rather than just react out of wounds.

> Once God healed my heart, I could respond to circumstances and not just react out of wounds.

Now when John calls me to tell me about delays, I can simply say, "Go be your patient's hero today!" No longer are my wounds projected onto the situation. I can see the situation for what it is: sick patients need his expertise, and it has nothing to do with me.

Learning about triggers and their value in deconstructing the false belief structures in our hearts is a beneficial component in exposing the Enemy's strongholds. We all have triggers, but hopefully you don't have as many as I did. Either way, I encourage you to pay attention to your reactions; if you find yourself going from zero to one hundred in short order, take note and ask God to help you understand why.

The Body Talks

We are triune beings. We have body, soul, and spirit. Understanding this truth is important since every aspect of our being is connected and provides us with significant clues as we seek to uncover areas in our heart that are under enemy domain. What affects your soul also affects your spirit and your body.

Dr. Dan Allender expresses it this way: "When the heart and mind and soul are injured, . . . we must recognize that the body was not on a protected island but was also injured and is likely still suffering."[25] In other words, our bodies, as well as our souls and spirits, carry injustices and wounds.

Professionals "have learned that trauma is not just an event that took place sometime in the past; it is also the imprint left by that experience on mind, brain, and *body*. This imprint has ongoing consequences for how the human organism manages to survive in the present" (emphasis mine).[26] Simply said, our bodies carry trauma and exhibit it in many ways—often through sickness.

Years ago, I attended a conference on the spiritual aspect of disease. It was an eye-opening experience. I had been trained medically as a nurse but had no awareness of the body-soul-spirit connection. Since attending that conference, I have heard many stories of people being healed from sickness after facing the emotional and spiritual issues from their past. I, too, experienced this.

For years, prior to God's healing, I had migraines every day and lived on ibuprofen. I had no idea that my background was affecting me physically, but as God progressively set me free from bondage, the migraines disappeared.

Along with exhibiting injury through sickness, our bodies can have sensory memories. I discovered this when I experienced unwarranted irrational anger when someone moved too close to me physically. I felt pressed in. This reaction left me confused.

The Lord later revealed to me that my body "remembered" being bound by the "therapist," and this experience represented a body memory. Is it any wonder why I had the feeling of claustrophobia? Although I minimized the effect of the "therapy" in my mind, my body continued to hint at the truth.

We have covered a lot of ground in this chapter, much of which was difficult. You might feel as if I opened a can of worms or how I felt when I began exploring my faulty foundation—when everything seemed like a jumbled-up bowl of spaghetti. It can be overwhelming and can leave one feeling hopeless.

However, be assured, no matter how much of our heart is under the influence of the Enemy, Christ has already procured our freedom and is committed to bringing us out of captivity and into His marvelous light (1 Peter 2:9). Please don't lose heart. In the next chapter, I'll focus more on how freedom is secured.

Weapons of Our Warfare

For though we walk in the flesh, we do not war according to the flesh. For the weapons of our warfare are not carnal but mighty in God for pulling down strongholds, casting down arguments and every high thing that exalts itself against the knowledge of God, bringing every thought into captivity to the obedience of Christ.
2 Corinthians 10:3–5 NKJV

From the moment we are saved until the moment we breathe our last breath, God, through the power of the Holy Spirit, works at making us into His image, thereby rendering the plan of the Enemy null and void.

There was a time when I didn't think God would do anything for me. I might have said a prayer for help, but I didn't really expect Him to help. Since I was coming from a victim mentality with low self-esteem born from lies, it is no wonder I had low expectations of God. It seemed easier to expect nothing from people or from God, because when I got nothing, disappointment was minimal.

This mindset is contrary to the reality and heart of God. Christ has given us the privilege of expecting Him to be true to His Word, His character, and His ways. As we leave the place of prayer and communion with Him after asking for His help, He wants us to consciously expect Him to hear our prayers and respond to them.

Don't get me wrong—God is not going to be manipulated. We can't expect Him to grant all our prayers exactly how we want them granted. The truth is that God does listen and He does respond with answers, but just not always how we think He should. Unfortunately, many people get upset with God or become disillusioned because God didn't answer the way they expected.

However, God loves you more than you could ever know, and He is even more committed to your well-being and growth than you are. He is invested in you. How do I know? He sacrificed what was dearest to Him—His Son—to guarantee your success.

> **We have to fight God's enemy-now our enemy too-right along with Him.**

There is one small detail, though, that we can't overlook. God doesn't do it all. He calls you to "work out your own salvation" too (Philippians 2:12). We are not called to passivity in our journey. We have to fight God's enemy, who is also our enemy, right along with Him.

Thankfully, God didn't leave us defenseless. He provided us with weapons. Of course, they are not physical weapons, but nonetheless they are mighty weapons for the warfare He has called us to. As we wield these weapons, God guarantees success and promises that all the power of heaven will back us up.

Decades ago, when I cried out for God's help as a desperate young woman, I never expected to embark on a journey similar to the character Much-Afraid in *Hinds' Feet on High Places*. I was as ignorant as she seemed to be, thinking the Lord would just zap and puff, and I would be magically healed and whole and become His exquisite image bearer instantly.

Come on! He's God. He can do it in the twinkling of an eye. What I didn't realize was that while God could do it, of course, it would not be best for me. Similarly, the Chief Shepherd could have transported Much-Afraid to the high places, but He knew it was best for her to make the journey herself. However, like God, He promised He would help her through.[27]

This is true for us too. God can do the miraculous for us, but He is more invested in what will help us in the long term so that we can effectively rule and reign with His Son. Therefore, He calls us as His partners on this journey toward growth in His character and ways. We do what we are able to do, and He in turn does what only He can do. The amazing thing about God is that He calls us to

God can do the miraculous for us, but He is more invested in what will develop us in the long term.

do our part on the journey, but He then provides all we need and enables us to actually do our part. His presence and resources are with us, but we must also actively engage in the battle for freedom.

God provides many weapons to help us do this. Picking up our weapons requires determination as well as a healthy dose of trust that God will make good on His word. I encourage you to trust God and expect this of Him. God desires to surprise us and to do "immeasurably more than all we ask or imagine" (Ephesians 3:20 NIV). Trust Him, for He is trustworthy.

Ultimately, the choice is yours, but I can assure you that what He has done for me, He will do for you. He won't fail you!

Steeped in Truth

I know I've talked at length about the Holy Spirit, but I just can't say enough about Him. Without Him on our journey, the battle would be impossible.

God is the One who knows you inside and out, and He has provided the greatest Counselor to guide us into all truth. He knows what damage the Enemy has wreaked. He knows our hearts, even when we don't. He knows what we believe and what we don't believe. We can trust Him and can interpret our memories, triggers, and behaviors much better with Him than without Him. We can trust Him to lead us, whether it's to a counselor or to any other form of assistance as He exposes the faulty belief structures of our hearts and imparts truth to us—truth that is absolute.

Back in the late 1980s, I had the privilege of hearing the Christian author Frank Peretti speak. He declared that in the years to come, truth would become relative; you have truth, and I have truth. Truth is what we decide it is. There is no absolute truth.

At the time, I thought he was crazy. Fast forward a few decades, and here we are. Truth has become relative. According to the Bible, this is impossible, for there is truth and there are lies. Truth is absolute and is found in God. All truth is God's truth. Period.

If we are to find truth, we need to rely on the Holy Spirit to reveal it to us.

Our interpretation of truth might be questionable, but God is truth. Unlike the yin and yang sign, there are no lies or evil in God. Therefore, if we are to find truth, we need to rely on the Holy Spirit to reveal it to us.

The primary way the Holy Spirit reveals truth is through the Word of God. He is quite adept at using it to uproot the deceptions of our hearts. We are assured that God's Word "is living and active, sharper than any two-edged sword, piercing to the division of soul and of spirit, of joints and of marrow, and discerning the thoughts and intentions of the heart" (Hebrews 4:12). The Word is the sword that we need in order to expose and tear down the lies that the Enemy has planted in our hearts. God's Word, His truth, powerfully exposes contrary belief structures that are securely hidden.

We are promised that the Word of God will be effective and won't return void (Isaiah 55:11). It will have its way and will fulfill the purpose God intends. From the beginning, God planned our lives to be founded in love and truth, so He lovingly commits to tear down all that is not properly constructed and to rebuild the faulty foundations hindering us. More often than not, we have no idea what is in our hearts, so we have to "let God and His Word straighten out our false beliefs."[28] If we do, God promises that we will experience the abundant life told of in His living Word.

I don't have to look far to see examples of God's Word at work. I'll never forget reading 1 Corinthians 13:4–8 as a young married woman. These verses, used often in marriage ceremonies, convey God's definition of love. The passage glaringly accentuated to me how impure my love was for my husband as well as how true love was meant to be expressed. The Word deeply convicted me. When I continued to fall short, the Holy Spirit lovingly reminded me by bringing those Bible verses back to my memory as He encouraged me to choose to walk in His love for my husband.

Another time, the Word of God helped me lose weight. I'm not kidding! I came across a verse, Proverbs 25:16, which essentially says, "Let me eat only what is sufficient for my body, lest I vomit."

Every time I opened the pantry door and reached for a snack, the Holy Spirit whispered, "Is this sufficient?" Invariably, the answer was no, and I would shut the door.

The Holy Spirit didn't leave it there but probed a little deeper, asking, "Why are you wanting to eat something?" Often, the answer was that I was bored or was emotionally eating, expecting food to make me feel better. Once the lie I believed about food being my healer was exposed, God could heal the pain and reveal Himself as the healer.

Through these and many other experiences, I personally learned that using the Word of God is powerful and is quite effective at revealing and correcting issues of the heart.

God's goal is to demolish any unholy strongholds the Enemy has formed in us and replace them with His truth. Once the stronghold lies have been revealed, it is critical to replace them with the truth.

I often imagine this process in terms of our hearts being like a computer running a program. Any programmer will tell you that when part of the system gets corrupted from bad data, the corrupted files have to be discovered and deleted. Once this is done, the computer can be reprogrammed with new data.

This analogy highlights why we can often read Scripture, learn it, and know it without it seeming to have any effect on our hearts. Our hearts contain corrupted data that interferes with the Word being established. Thus, it is essential for us to allow the Holy Spirit to expose and heal anything in our hearts that is not based on God's truth so that the ground of our hearts will be fertile for the implantation of His Word. At this point, meditating on the truth will bring life and change.

Casting Down Arguments

We have learned that strongholds are built upon a bed of lies. The lies take hold of our hearts when we receive them and perpetually rehearse them back to ourselves. It often takes years for the Enemy to complete our bondage. It all started with a sin—our own or another person's sin against us—and progressed to false thoughts that we believed. Once we agreed with the lies, they started

Once the stronghold-lies have been revealed, it is critical to replace them with the truth.

to shape our decisions, which then affected our actions, our values, and our lifestyle, ultimately solidifying our bondage.[29]

To uncover the original lie and perpetrated sin, the Holy Spirit encourages us to examine our lifestyle, values, actions, and the decisions we have made. Sometimes it seems as if you are following endless trails to discover your internalized lies.

Finding freedom from my low self-esteem issues seemed like a never-ending process. It was clear that I believed I was "less than" and worthless, but it seemed as if it took forever to heal. There were so many elements that ingrained this lie into my heart.

As the Holy Spirit took me down memory lane, I journaled and mentally noted how each experience had wedged this lie deeper and deeper. Finally, I came to the memory when, as a toddler, I was literally told, "You are worthless!" I had internalized this lie as truth and had believed it. From that point on, my life and self-worth were shaped and filtered through the lie. It didn't matter how many times I read Bible verses about who I was in Christ; the lie was so thoroughly embedded in my soul that God's Word never got through.

The problem was that I believed it! Subconsciously, I rehearsed it over and over in my mind. Through that lie, the Enemy had an open door to continue working it in and building upon it. It completely infected my life like an unseen abscess. Anytime I wasn't picked on a team, I heard the lie. Anytime I was seemingly ignored, I heard the lie. Anytime I didn't do things right, I heard the lie. The lie filled my head and had free rent to reside there—and I allowed it.

Yes, I was a little girl when it began, but anytime we believe the lies and continue in them, God calls it sin. Does He understand that my abuser planted the lie? Yes. However, I agreed with it for decades. I was complicit. Thankfully, God, in His love, made a weapon for us so we could be free from the lies and sin that have bound us. That weapon is repentance!

Christ, by His death on the cross, provided for forgiveness of sin once and for all (Hebrews 10:12–14). Every sin we've ever committed is forgiven. However, we have to actuate this forgiveness by seeing our sins (in this case, the lies I believed) and placing them on the cross.

When I teach this lesson, I find it helpful for people to do an experiential exercise as they repent for the lies they have believed. Each person spends time alone with God confessing the lies they have believed and asking for forgiveness for living in agreement with the lies. When they are finished praying, I have them write the lies on a small piece of paper and tack the paper on a homemade cross, demonstrating that the lies are taken care of by the cross.

The exercise often becomes a significant visual marker of the spiritual transaction that has occurred—walking away free from the lies and captivity. God's Word promises, "If we confess our sins, he is faithful and just to forgive us our sins and to cleanse us from all unrighteousness" (1 John 1:9).

As an illustration, I've displayed examples of some of the faulty mindsets I have repented of:

Repentance is more than just confessing sin and asking for forgiveness. It is also falling out of agreement with the lie and then coming into agreement with God's truth.

I love how simply my friend Janice says it: *I am wrong, God, and You are right!*

God is right. His truth is right. The lies we believed are wrong.

Coming into agreement with God will require more than just believing; it will also necessitate action. All our behaviors and actions resulting from the lie must be changed. This is where the Word of God and actions go hand in hand. Just as the stronghold was born out of a lie, so the truth implanted and meditated on over and over will be planted deeply in our cleansed hearts.

Once we have repented and replaced the lie with God's Word, we need to turn away and change our decisions and behavior so they line up with the truth. As we do, the power plug of the Enemy is pulled out. We cast down his arguments, and Satan loses his influence.

I've Got to Do What? Forgive?

Another powerful tool God provides is the weapon of forgiveness. I can almost hear the gasps. Forgiveness is not a popular topic, yet it is critical to walking in freedom. If part of our destiny is to be God's image bearers, we can't get away from the fact that one facet of God's character is forgiveness. I am glad this is true, for when we were dead in our sins and rebellion, God was merciful and forgave us our sins, seating us in the heavenly realms with Christ (Ephesians 2:1–6).

Being like Christ, we must then be forgiving. He commands it (Ephesians 4:32; Colossians 3:13). When asked by Peter how many times we are required to forgive, Jesus replied, "Seventy times seven" (Matthew 18:21–22 kjv). That's a lot of forgiveness.

The thing about forgiveness is that it actually frees us and keeps us from bitterness. We can often misunderstand why God tells us to do something, forgetting that everything He does is with a heart of selfless love for our own good. Forgiveness is not just for the good of others, but it

> **The thing about forgiveness is that it actually frees us and keeps us from bitterness.**

is also for our own good. God is not asking us to do something He hasn't already done. He asks it of us so we can walk in freedom, cutting off the ball and chain that binds us to those who have hurt us.

118

I can admit that this was a tough one for me. It was easy to forgive little things, such as when someone said something unintentionally hurtful to me. Forgive them? No problem! However, when it came to forgiving my father and my abuser—that was a different matter.

There was nothing in me that wanted to forgive them. However, forgiveness has nothing to do with feelings. It is a commandment, and choosing to obey is simply an act of the will. Our will is the part of us that chooses; I can either choose or not.

When it came to forgiving my father, I wrestled a bit, but then I chose to forgive him. I prayed and told the Lord I forgave him. The Lord's simple reply was, "For what?"

Lord! You know everything!

Of course He did, but He wanted to teach me something, so He impressed upon me to write a list of all the ways my father had hurt me. Everything I held against him—even those things I needed from him, such as attention—was to be placed on the list. The Lord wanted me to know exactly what the debt was that my father owed me, and thus what I needed to forgive him for.

After I finished the list, the Lord told me to burn it as an act of forgiveness.

Now wait a minute, Lord. Isn't that going a bit too far?

His reply was, "No. Burn it."

I cried over that list for more than an hour before I could burn it. Once I did, though, forgiveness for Dad washed over me, and I experienced a sense of release and freedom.

There are other times, however, when forgiving someone seems downright impossible. That was how I felt in regard to my sexual abuser. Nothing in me wanted to forgive him. I couldn't even drum it up in my will. Finally, all I could pray was, *Lord, I am willing to be made willing to forgive him.*

I probably shouldn't admit this, but it took years for me to actually forgive him. However, God was faithfully at work in me in the midst of my pain until I willingly forgave my abuser, despite still feeling a deep resistance.

Why was it so hard to forgive him? That man hurt me to the core of my being, and not only did he hurt me, but he indirectly hurt my husband and children as well. In my mind, forgiving him meant that he was off the hook. I failed to understand that forgiveness didn't mean he wouldn't face God for what he had done. Forgiveness just meant I had released him to God.

My pastor and friend, Joe Daltorio, explained forgiveness in a way that shifted my understanding. He said, "Forgiveness is taking yourself off the judge's seat and letting God be in His rightful place as judge."

I realized I had been sitting in the judge's seat and was convicting my perpetrator rather than trusting him to God. Wow! I certainly didn't want to be the judge and walk in mistrust of God. God's goodness and love amaze me. He knew and understood my struggle in forgiving this man.

Later, as a friend was helping me walk through the final release of this man, God gave me a picture to help me release him forever. As I was speaking about forgiveness, I saw in my spirit a rowboat tethered to a dock. Two Roman soldiers came up to me, and as I forgave this man, they took hold of his arms and placed him in the boat. I saw myself push the boat away from the dock, and it disappeared. God, in His kindness, understood the importance of justice to me, and He gave me this vision to confirm that justice would be served.

The crazy thing about forgiveness and the vision God gave me is that it actually engendered mercy toward my abuser. He was already dead, but I prayed for mercy for him. The ball and chain I had lugged around for decades was removed. I was free, and I looked a tiny bit more like my Savior.

I'm sure that for many of you, forgiveness seems like an insurmountable obstacle. It certainly seemed like it to me. The Lord, however, is with us and enables us to do everything He asks us to—even if it takes years, if we need a vision, or if we have to write a list of our grievances so we can ultimately burn it up and forgive. The God who calls us to Himself doesn't just give us a stone tablet of "Thou shalt nots." Certainly not. He gives us the strength and the ability to do what He asks of us.

If you have someone you need to forgive, make a choice to walk in obedience to God's Word, asking God to help you walk fully in forgiveness so you can experience freedom.

Obedience: The Fuel for Transformation

Speaking about obedience—we had to get here sooner or later. It is another dreaded word, yet it is a word that represents a powerful weapon the Enemy hates, and from which miracles are birthed.

I love the Bible because it is chock-full of lively stories of regular people like you and me for whom crazy things happen when they walk in obedience. Think about Moses, who took one million Israelites out from under their captor. He considered himself a nobody, yet his obedience brought freedom for the multitude. His obedience to lift his arms at God's command parted the Red Sea so all his countrymen could pass through to safety. Obedience. It is very difficult at times, but the benefit is unmistakable.

My dear friend Dave Buehring has a simple equation that points to the truth borne out in Scripture: "Revelation plus obedience equals transformation."[30] I love this. It makes it so clear. When God gives us revelation about something, such as lies, there is almost always a point of obedience He is calling us to take. If we walk in obedience to the revelation, God promises that He will bring transformation.

If we walk in obedience to the revelation, God promises He'll bring transformation.

Years ago, I was spending time in prayer, and out of the blue, I sensed the Holy Spirit telling me, "You place a big stamp of failure on everything your mother does. You have stamped her as a failure as a mother."

I pondered this revelation and knew that the Holy Spirit only speaks truth. He then told me to call my mom and ask for forgiveness. That was my obedience point. I could choose to obey or not. I chose to listen and obey. I was surprised at what followed.

I called my mom and told her what the Holy Spirit had revealed to me. I asked her for forgiveness. What she said next gave me a new insight into bondage. After forgiving me, she exclaimed, "You know, now that I think about it, I did that to my mother, and she did that to her mother."

Again, revelation was given. I realized it was a generational pattern unknowingly handed down. It was an unwanted gift that kept on giving. My spirit rose up and said, "No. It ends here!" I have a daughter, and I was not about to see that gift handed down to her. I prayed against it and spiritually broke the pattern.

The transformation resulted in my daughter and me having an amazing relationship. She is one of my dearest friends. Who knows how it would have turned out if I had not obeyed the revelation the Holy Spirit had lovingly given to me?

A life of obedience not only sets the stage for transformation, but it also reveals our love and trust for God. Years ago, Gary Chapman wrote a book called *The Five Love Languages*. It gives an insightful exploration of how people receive love. The Bible makes it very clear that God's love language is obedience. A few Bible verses highlight this truth:

> Samuel said, "Has the Lord as great delight in burnt offerings and sacrifices, as in obeying the voice of the Lord? Behold, to obey is better than sacrifice, and to listen than the fat of rams." (1 Samuel 15:22)

> If you love me, you will keep my commandments. (John 14:15)

> If anyone loves me, he will keep my word, and my Father will love him, and we will come to him and make our home with him. (John 14:23)

> This is love, that we walk according to his commandments; this is the commandment, just as you have heard from the beginning, so that you should walk in it. (2 John 1:6)

God makes it clear that those who obey Him are showing that they love Him. All too often, Christians fall into the trap of believing they have to sacrifice time, treasure, and talent to reveal their love for God. I don't deny that a life of following Christ involves sacrifice and service, but it is a life of obedience that touches the heart of God, routs the Enemy, and brings transformative power to our lives.

Walking with Humility

It is difficult to imagine that humility is a weapon God calls us to use in our journey toward freedom and sanctification, but it is. God calls us to be humble as He is humble.

Christ was the embodiment of this quality, as communicated in Philippians, and we are encouraged to follow His example (Philippians 2:3–8). This passage says that Christ, who created the universe with the Father, who is the Prince of Peace, and who sits on the right hand of the Father, came humbly as a baby, unable to do anything for Himself, and did only what the Father told Him to do. He walked the earth and willingly laid down His life, dying on the cross for you and for me. Humility is His very nature, and as His image bearers, He requires nothing less of us.

Humility battles the Enemy and resists his plan.

Humility battles the Enemy and resists his plan. Satan is the complete antithesis of humility. One of his tactics is to draw us away from God through pride. When I think of pride, the image of a boastful, full-of-himself person comes to mind. That is certainly one face of pride—a blatant face for sure. However, pride can be more insidious, making it harder to detect. It can manifest as an overfocus on self or always making things about you. Pride, in whatever form, steals the glory from God and takes it for ourselves. It helps puff us up and makes us feel good about ourselves.

Regrettably, I am all too familiar with pride. Growing up with low self-esteem, I subconsciously used thoughts and behaviors that would build me up so I wouldn't feel so bad about myself.

I mentioned earlier that I was a people person. Part of my observations would be turned into pride: "I would never do that." "I do that better than they do." "My family's not that bad." These are the kinds of messages I would tell myself in order to try to feel better.

The ugly truth is that it was pride. James 4:6 tells us that "God opposes the proud but gives grace to the humble." When I discovered this verse, the Holy Spirit began to illuminate to me the pride pattern of my heart. There was no denying it. I proceeded to humble myself by agreeing with Him, repenting, asking for forgiveness, and allowing Him to heal the root of my insecurities.

However, it didn't stop there. I had to continually walk in humility by being aware of my thoughts, capturing any prideful ones that popped up, and repenting quickly for them. After a while of doing this, the thoughts diminished and I was no longer plagued by them.

Years ago, I found out that humility wasn't exactly modeled to me as a Christian. A classic example of people trying to be humble is when gifted people are complimented about their gifts. Often, their immediate reply as they back away is, "No, no, no. It's not me. It's all God! Glory to God."

This reaction always felt off to me. Something just didn't sit well. It wasn't until my friend Dave Buehring explained his definition of humility that understanding dawned on me. He clarified that "humility is being willing to be known for who you really are,"[31] both for your strengths and for your weaknesses.

Therefore, humility is acknowledging who God has made us to be as well as acknowledging who we aren't and what our weaknesses and shortcomings are. Christ certainly reflected this to us, although He was devoid of weaknesses. I think of how He walked and engaged with people. He knew who He was and didn't need to push Himself forward or prove to anyone who He was. That is humility!

> Humility is being willing to be known for who you really are—Dave Buehring

I have often thought of Dave's definition when someone compliments me on something such as my singing voice: *Be willing to be known for who you really are.* My new response is, "Thank you so much. It's a gift God gave me, and I'm so touched that He used it to minister to you."

I think of this definition when something is pointed out to me that is not so pretty in myself: *Be willing to be known for who you really are.* I have to own it and say, "Yes, I did that, and I am so sorry. Will you forgive me? I'm weak in this area. Please pray for me."

This side of humility is more challenging since it makes us vulnerable. However, God calls us to walk humbly, and He promises that He will exalt us if we do (James 4:10). God will lift us up and help us overcome the Enemy with humility.

God gives us weapons to use so that the territory of our hearts that is held captive by the Enemy can be recaptured and surrendered to Christ. God will do His part in freeing us, but we need to partner with Him and fulfill our responsibilities as well. God has already secured our victory. All we have to do is deploy the weapons He has given us. The Holy Spirit will lead us in the use of these weapons, and He will help us so we can gain our freedom back.

Part 3

Reclaiming
What
Was Stolen

A Restored, Resurrected Heart

*After you have suffered a little while,
the God of all grace, who has called you
to his eternal glory in Christ,
will himself restore, confirm, strengthen,
and establish you.*
1 Peter 5:10

Restoration. What a wonderful word! It is a promise given by God that speaks volumes to a broken heart that has seen much suffering.

Sadly, we live in a fallen world, and suffering will touch our lives. It will affect some people more than others. Some people will suffer for the cause of Christ, although it is undeniable that all will be forced to endure some level of pain, distress, or turmoil. It's inevitable.

Maybe "forced" is not completely true, as our suffering is sometimes brought on by our own poor choices. No matter the cause, suffering will come. That's why I love the verse above from 1 Peter. It gives me hope in the midst of my suffering; things will not always be this way. God promises restoration.

I love *Merriam-Webster*'s definition of restoration: "A bringing back to a former position or condition."[32] That's what we want, right? We want to be brought back to God's original condition for mankind. At least that is what I want! I want everything God intended from the beginning—pre-enemy interference. Yes, I want restoration from all the ways the enemy has infiltrated my life and caused pain, suffering, and long-lasting repercussions.

As someone who loves to study the Bible, I enjoy looking at the original Greek and Hebrew meanings of biblical words. Sometimes our English language just doesn't cut it. I knew what *Merriam-Webster* said, but I was curious to see if the original language added insight. I found words such as mend, repair, complete, put in order, arrange, strengthen, perfect, and make one what he ought to be. My goodness! That was exactly the process God was doing in me. The words not only described what God was doing, but they described where He was taking me.

As I was thinking about suffering, another Bible passage popped into my head: "That I may know him and the power of his resurrection, and may share his sufferings, becoming like him in his death, that by any means possible I may attain the resurrection from the dead" (Philippians 3:10–11).

Yes, there it was again. *Suffering.* Not just ours, but also Christ's. Christ was well acquainted with suffering; His suffering led to death. Sometimes our sufferings lead to death too—the death of our hearts.

Our dead and captive hearts God can resurrect to life; restoring and bringing them to their original design.

Paul says that when we suffer, we share in Christ's sufferings. He follows with a parallel: just as Christ suffered and was resurrected, we too, suffer and can be resurrected. We are promised that the same power that raised Christ from the dead will also raise us from the dead. God can resurrect our dead and captive hearts to life, restoring them and bringing them to their original design.

When the Holy Spirit revealed this to me, I found it to be such good news! It wasn't a reality then, but it was certainly a promise to hang on to.

Throughout the years, my heart has soared in gratitude for how God has been fulfilling this promise. When I first stepped into this journey, which I now know is called sanctification—the process of Christ making me more into His image—I had no idea what a restored heart would look like. Over time, the Holy Spirit gave me firsthand experience, and I have seen in myself many manifestations of a restored, resurrected heart, one that progressively reflects God's image more visibly.

Less of Me and More of Him

Having walked with the Lord for a while, I have learned that one of the manifestations of a restored heart is a growing desire to be filled more with God than with myself. I often ponder John the Baptist's declaration: "He must increase, but I must decrease" (John 3:30). I know John was talking about his earthly ministry and the rise of Christ's ministry, but a spiritual analogy beckons my heart as well: Christ in me increasing and me decreasing.

It's not that I want to lose who I am, for God formed me with a specific personality, abilities, and giftings. These don't change. However, what my restored heart is pining for is for Christ and His ways to shine more brightly so that I don't taint and dull His expression by my fleshly, earthly tendencies.

What my restored heart is pining for is Christ and His ways to shine more brightly.

From the onset of my journey, the prayers of my heart have been simple: "Search me, O God, and know my heart! Try me and know my thoughts! And see if there be any grievous way in me, and lead me in the way everlasting" (Psalm 139:23–24); and "Create in me a clean heart, O God, and renew a right spirit within me. . . . Restore to me the joy of your salvation, and uphold me with a willing spirit" (Psalm 51:10, 12).

When I first voiced these prayers, I had no idea what the answer would entail or that the dysfunction of my background had invaded my heart, filling it with junk and distorting the personality and gifts that God had placed to display Himself through me.

Being a young, immature Christian, I thought Christianity was all about performing to please God. I tried desperately to be a good Christian woman, doing all the right things and trying to behave according to the Word of God. I never guessed that I was projecting a wounded-childhood, good-girl mentality onto my concept of Christianity.

It wasn't until years later that I realized I was living under the Old Testament law of performance to try to obtain right standing with God rather than living under grace and the redemption Christ had obtained for me. I had no idea that Christ had freed me from the law's bondage and that the gospel was about "Christ in you, the hope of glory" (Colossians 1:27).

I later learned the truth. Salvation by performance, or the law, had been abolished at the cross. It wasn't meant to save or transform people. Redemption through Christ and His Spirit's continuing work in me was the only way to the heart transformation my prayers asked for.

Self-effort through performance does nothing. Only Christ in me brought the hope of true restoration.

Self-effort through performance does nothing. Only Christ in me brought the hope of true restoration.

As I realized this, I felt horrible. I felt like an idiot. Being clueless, I had inadvertently placed a yoke of slavery on myself and my family, forcing us into a Christian box of performance. I had not only hurt my family, but I had nearly destroyed myself. Desperate for Christ's character in me, I continued my silent prayers, adding, *More of You, Jesus; more of You in my heart.*

The Lord faithfully began exposing and tearing down the walls of my "box" and heart. The more He did so, the more I discovered who I was and the more I noticed Him shining more brilliantly through me.

Thinking about Christ increasing in me and me becoming less, my mind drifts to the process of refining gold. This is a process in which gold is heated to high temperatures, forcing the impurities to the surface so they can be skimmed off. The process continues until all the impurities are gone—until the refiner looks into the liquid gold and can see his face clearly reflected back.

This process mirrors what Christ has done and continues to do in my heart. He takes out impurities so His image is more accurately reflected. More of Him and less of me!

A restored heart willingly submits to this refining work of Christ, deeply desiring continued purification so as to more clearly display Christ's character and ways to the world.

Abundant Fruit

One result of God resurrecting my heart was an amazing transformation as He exhibited more of His fruit in my life. The fruit I'm talking about isn't found in a grocery store. It is spiritual: love, joy, peace, patience, kindness, goodness, faithfulness, gentleness, and self-control (Galatians 5:22–23). This fruit is willingly and liberally imparted by the Spirit who dwells in us.

However, if our hearts are filled with other things, the full display of His fruit is made difficult. Thinking back to the "Ice Queen" days of my life, although I know people saw spiritual fruit in me, I experienced a lot of other "fruit" swirling around inside me—and it was definitely not fruit that was given by the Spirit.

You may know what I'm speaking of. I am talking about the fruit of the sinful nature—the flesh—things such as impurity, hostility, quarreling, jealousy, selfish ambition, envy, and division. This is the fruit we try to hide—or at least I did.

Growing up, I tried being perfect and a good girl. This "bad" fruit was definitely not part of being good, so I worked diligently to suppress it. However, I could sure smell it, and it was putrid. Unfortunately, the people I loved the most (my husband and my children) smelled the fruit too. I didn't intend for them to, but my triggers tripped me up every time, and in the height of emotion, I had a hard time hiding my fleshly fruit. Let's be honest: I stunk at it (no pun intended).

That is why I am so thankful for a restored heart. God dealt with much of my baggage and healed many of my triggers and wounds, enabling the Spirit to more effortlessly flow through my heart and exhibit His fruit. With restoration, I no longer had to try to manufacture good fruit through self-effort, which had been exhausting.

With restoration, I no longer had to try to manufacture good fruit through self-efforts, which had been exhausting.

In my experience, people around us can tell when fruit is real and when it is manufactured. I'm sure you've seen people with manufactured smiles plastered on their faces and trying to act all nice and sweet. You likely have seen people who perpetually wear a congenial mask, but when they think no one's looking, they let their true colors show: manufactured fruit.

The saying "Fake it until you make it" is a bunch of hot air. You can't manufacture or fake genuine spiritual fruit. Have you ever seen a fruit tree labor hard to produce fruit? No! The fruit is naturally produced by the tree. Trust me—we can't produce spiritual fruit by sheer willpower either. I know this because I spent years trying to fake good fruit, but I learned that what did not exist in my heart could not be produced by repetition. Christ's declaration that "out of the abundance of the heart the mouth speaks" (Matthew 12:34) proved altogether too true for me.

Although my heart was filled with much good fruit, my wounds spoke far more loudly to me in my early days through the ugly fruit of insecurity, jealousy, envy, selfishness, and anger. My heart was filled with splashes of jealousy and envy of other people's nuclear families, including their money, their homes, their abilities and talents, the grades they received, and how smart they were. It went on and on and on ad nauseam.

Additionally, because my heart suffered with insecurity, whatever anyone did became about me. All my focus was wretchedly on self and how far short I fell. All my negative experiences colored my failings, no matter if they were real or imagined: *I* was defective. *I* was rejectable. *I* was bad. As you can see, it was bad, decaying, rotten fruit. It was nothing like what the Spirit had for me.

Thankfully, heart restoration removes the rotten fruit and replaces it with the luscious fruit of the Spirit. A restored, resurrected heart is one that has been put back to the way it was supposed to be. It is a heart that is mended, repaired, complete, and perfect. In other words, the person is back to being how God first intended, progressively walking in and exhibiting the Spirit's fruit.

The emergence of Spirit fruit from a restored heart makes life's journey and sanctification well worth the challenges of pursuing truth.

The emergence of the fruit of the Spirit from a restored heart makes life's journey and sanctification well worth the challenges of pursuing truth. God has been restoring this fruit in my heart, and He promises to restore it in yours.

Embracing True Identity

Having a restored heart also means embracing the identity Christ has obtained for you. The Bible is overflowing with verses that give a clear indication of who we are in Christ—our true identity. Observe what is revealed in the Bible about our identity:

- I am a member of a chosen race, a royal priesthood, a holy nation, a people for His own possession, that you may proclaim the excellencies of Him who called you out of darkness into His marvelous light. (1 Peter 2:9)
- Since you are His child, God has also made you an heir. (Galatians 4:7)
- I am a holy person. (Ephesians 1:1)
- I am seated in the heavenly realm, with Christ, in all His authority over Satan's kingdom. (Ephesians 1:19–23; 2:5–6)
- I am holy and share in the heavenly calling. (Hebrews 3:1)
- I am God's temple, and God's Spirit dwells in me. (1 Corinthians 3:16)
- I am God's child, His heir, and a co-heir with Christ. (Romans 8:16–17)
- I am loved by God and am a saint. (Romans 1:7)

This represents only a smattering of verses written about those who are in Christ. They signify how God sees us and how we will begin seeing ourselves once we are restored and agree with what God says. Did you ever think you were holy and a saint? I certainly didn't think I was until I received the truth of God's Word.

Unfortunately, too many of us in Christ are living under a false identity—an identity developed by the lies we've agreed with for years. All too often, we see ourselves through the filter of our strongholds, and we deem what we see as our identity. This is false!

For years, I saw myself in faulty ways. Do you remember the weeds

God showed me that were growing up and covering the beautiful garden He had planted in me? One of those weeds was the belief that I was stupid. I don't remember being called that or anything like it. The only thing I remember is the academic struggle I had with English and history. Regardless, the lie was deeply embedded in my soul, and it shaped my identity.

No matter how irrational, the lie was truth to me, and my self-talk confirmed it over and over. Even when I was ranked sixth out of one hundred in my high school graduating class, the truth didn't sink in. Consequently, many of the decisions I made stemmed from that lie. Thinking I was too stupid to succeed in a four-year college, I attended a diploma nursing school instead. This mindset made no sense because nursing school was equally challenging. However, my identity was influenced by that lie as well as by many others. These lies created an identity that was erroneous and had nothing to do with truth.

Obviously, we now recognize that God doesn't want us to go through life captive to lies and strongholds and not knowing who we are. Whether we grasp the truth about who we are or not doesn't make God's truth any less real.

As God began to pull the weeds of false identity, the truth of my identity as reflected in His Word slowly seeped in.

Once I became a believer, my identity was immediately changed. The above verses are a handful of verses that describe who I became in that instant. In a transformative moment, I became God's daughter and an heir with Christ. However, I didn't comprehend this reality. My heart was polluted with the stuff of life, which made it difficult to fully receive the truth. As God began to pull the weeds of false identity from my heart, the truth of my identity as reflected in His Word slowly seeped in. Thankfully, as we receive His restorative healing, we can receive a greater revelation of who we are in Christ.

Like me, you may have weeds hindering your grasp of identity. Since the journey is lifelong, it is good that God never gets weary of setting us free. Despite having worked on me for years, God faithfully continues to touch any elusive, inaccurate mindset that remains.

God recently illuminated one of these. For most of my life, I struggled to feel like a valid part of anything, whether church, family, ministry—you name it. In my eyes, I never measured up. Seeking the Lord often, I asked Him why I had this irrational feeling.

Through circumstances, God answered my prayers by revealing my mindset's origin: illegitimacy! He showed me how the wound of illegitimacy prevented me from ever feeling that I belonged or was a legitimate member of anything. Consequently, I diligently worked to prove myself worthy. This buried root resulted in an excruciating internal battle that was being unwittingly waged for legitimacy. Thankfully, God opened my eyes to the truth and made a way for healing so that I could embrace my true identity as a beloved, accepted daughter.

As I read the Bible, it is clear to me that I'm not the only one who has dealt with false identity. Think of the story of Gideon. Imagine the scene when he is working and the angel of the Lord suddenly appears and calls out to him, "O mighty man of valor" (Judges 6:12), and then tells him to fight the Midianites!

Gideon told the Lord that he was from the weakest Israelite tribe and so was unqualified and unable to lead the fight. Oh, Gideon! Did he really believe that God didn't already know all about him? Sadly, he saw himself as weak. He had no idea what God saw in him or what God had in store for him. He had identity issues!

Lest we think Gideon was alone in his struggles, a dive into the Bible reveals that plenty of other people had the same struggle. What about Moses? Can you think of others?

Without a restored, resurrected heart, it's hard to see who we are. I want to assure you that Christ not only redeemed us so we would have a restored relationship with God and would be able to spend eternity with the Trinity, but He came to restore our original identity—an identity found in Him.

At this point, I feel like jumping up and shouting, "Hallelujah!" God has set us free from walking under a false identity, and He has procured a glorious identity for us as a son or

God has set us free from walking under a false identity,

daughter. This is good news! We no longer need to be weighed down by who we thought we were. Instead, we can embrace our true identity as a result of a restored and resurrected heart!

Lordship and Letting Go of Idols

When we truly give our hearts to Christ, He becomes the Lord of our lives—completely. Those whose hearts have been restored and resurrected desire the Lord to be, well—Lord. Restored individuals surrender completely, holding nothing back and not allowing their affection to be on anything but Christ. They recognize that He gave His life for them to be made alive.

Therefore, in order for Christ to be Lord and to have free rein in our lives, our hearts need to be completely abandoned to Him. When we make an initial decision for Christ, our intention is to give Christ full control of our hearts. However, whether through ignorance or immaturity, we often hinder His free access.

What frequently occurs instead is highlighted in Robert Boyd Munger's pamphlet, "My Heart—Christ's Home."[33] The author gives a poignant analogy of our heart being like a house where we let Christ into many rooms, but certainly do not want Him opening up the closet where we hide the unmentionables and what is rotten.

I love this story. It reveals so clearly what many of us do unintentionally—hiding our "nasties" away, thinking Christ isn't aware of what is hidden in the depths of our heart. The truth is that He already knows it all. Instead of turning to Him with our wounds, pain, and lies, we often turn to other things for comfort. These are the things idols are made of.

Idols! What are we talking about? We don't have idols, do we? Idols are those things that are substituted for or looked to instead of God, such as the golden calf or Dagon or Buddha. We are well aware that those idols are prohibited. The Bible makes it abundantly clear that they are sinful and should be turned away from (Exodus 20:3–5; Leviticus 19:4; 2 Kings 21:11; Psalm 106:36).

The sad truth is that most of us have idols. They may not appear as they did in the Old Testament, but invariably we have an unredeemed tendency to turn to idols for protection and comfort from our wounds. We don't intend to turn to anything other than God, but we do.

I know—I didn't want to admit it either. However, if we want to have a restored heart, we need to at least explore the possibility that we may have embraced an idol or two.

Most of us have idols.

To increase our understanding, let's look at what an idol really is. We're not talking about the physical and tangible ones the Israelites possessed but rather the secret and soul idols. Dee Brestin quotes David Clarkson as defining these idols as "when the mind and heart is set on anything more than God; when anything is more valued than God, more trusted . . . more loved."[34] Don't you hate that word "anything"? An idol is anything we turn to instead of God.

We may deny them, but if we ask God, what would He say? I tend to agree with Ms. Brestin: "All of us have hidden idols that need to be revealed, removed, and replaced. Christians who talk as if they have arrived may be the most blind of all."[35] We don't want to be blind. We are striving for restored and resurrected hearts, so we need to be courageous and aggressively face any potential personal idols head-on.

At this point, if you are anything like me, you may be wondering, "What kinds of things is she talking about? What could I be making into an idol?"

Here are just a few things that could be named: television, movies, money, social media (ouch), hobbies, food, or exercise. Let's go a little deeper and be a little more personal: parents, spouses, children, friends, alcohol, gambling, pets, and of course, drugs. I may have stepped on a few toes. Seriously, mine have already been trampled. I have had many idols in my life, and I may unsuspectingly have more.

A dog was probably the earliest idol I had as a child. Our family pet was always there to bring comfort and attention. Other idols in my life have included:

- My mother: I always looked to her for approval.
- Food: I was definitely an emotional eater.
- Friends: They minimized my loneliness and provided distraction.

- Books: They transported me from hurt and deposited me into another life.
- My husband: My wounded heart made John my knight in shining armor. My restored heart placed him rightly. He was always my knight—just not in God's place.
- Service to others: It made me feel useful and better about myself.

Anything can be an idol if we put it in God's place. Looking at the above list, I need to clarify something. All those things are made and given by God to be a blessing. The problem arises when we turn to those things instead of to God to soothe our hearts.

God blessed me greatly when He brought John Hodgson into my life. He desired us to walk together intimately and in supportive partnership. However, when I turned to John to fix my issues instead of turning to God, I unknowingly asked John to take the place of God, and that was a place that was impossible for him to take. It was unfair and wrong for me to do that to him.

Walking in restoration and resurrection will require each of us to confront harbored idols. The most beneficial way to identify them is to courageously ask the Holy Spirit to clearly reveal anything and everything we unwittingly put in God's place. Doing so, along with repenting and resolutely turning away from idols cleanses us and gives Christ greater room in our hearts. Ultimately, He is the only One who is trustworthy and capable of bringing the restoration we desire—unlike the idols we unknowingly or knowingly turn to instead.

Our resurrected hearts come to life after we put to death anything that keeps Christ from being Lord and having free rein.

Twinklings of Destiny

As we near the close of this chapter, it will be beneficial to briefly explore the effect of a restored and resurrected heart in discovering its destiny. Many people who read this book are actively engaged in doing what God has called them to. For me, and maybe for others, discovery of God's destiny is a process that unfolds over many years.

Before we go any further, let's recall a basic biblical truth: our corporate destiny is: first, to know God and walk in intimacy with Him and second, to make Him known and be His image bearers to the world. Each of us is called to this purpose.

However, in order for us to fulfill this destiny, God uniquely and specifically wires us to reflect Him in our specific circles of influence. Restored hearts discover how they are designed to walk in the specific destiny God originally intended.

Restored hearts discover how they are designed and walk in the specific destiny God originally intended.

As a child, I thought my destiny was to be a nurse, helping people heal from all their hurts. After giving my heart to the Lord and walking with Him for a while, I realized that nursing was *my* plan, but it didn't necessarily manifest God's plan and purpose. What was conceived when I was a child by my wounded heart and immature processing was leading me down the wrong life path. I was determined to keep others from hurting like I did. I was a good nurse, but that wasn't God's intent for me.

It wasn't until later, when I was a young mother, that I learned that God specifically and uniquely fashions us for His plan. I certainly could have remained a nurse. It is a noble calling, and God worked through me. Nevertheless, I suspect that eventually I wouldn't have been as fulfilled as I am now doing the ministry for which God uniquely wired me.

With the call to ministry firmly seeded in my heart, I enrolled in a leadership class. The nine-month leadership course encouraged exploration of several aspects pertaining to destiny, many of which I found eye-opening. In exploring and uncovering God's plan for your life, these elements may be beneficial to you as well.

One important evolving discovery was a fresh exploration and clearer comprehension of my spiritual gifts. There are many different spiritual-gift tests available. If you've never taken one, I would encourage you to do so. I discovered that as my heart was restored, the gifts I exhibited were more accurately expressed.

For example, as a young adult, prior to healing, I tested high in the spiritual gift of service. With God's healing, I realized my tendency toward service was based more in pleasing people than a reflection of a true spiritual gift. Of course, God wants His children to be servant-hearted, but having a servant's heart is quite different from having the spiritual gift of service. Resurrected hearts display spiritual gifts authentically rather than as a consequence of soul wounds.

Another exploration I found beneficial in detecting God's plan for me was to look at the things I naturally excelled in. I looked at talents I'd had from birth as well as those I had acquired throughout my life. Exploring these abilities provides valuable clues when determining God's purpose and destiny for us.

An illustration of a natural ability is my singing voice. God gifted me with a good voice, and I have a passion for singing, so it is a no-brainer for me to participate on a worship team. Also, I naturally have a passion and love for relating to and working with people. I can easily sit for hours listening to and caring for people.

As I assessed my abilities and makeup, I was amazed to realize how perfectly God had designed me for ministry. As an ambivert, I was formed by God to love being with people, like an extrovert, but also to enjoy solitude and pursuing God, like an introvert.

In contrast to natural abilities, there are other abilities I have had to acquire. One of these is my ability to speak publicly. Having lost my voice as a child, I was much happier fading into the woodwork. However, the fear of speaking hindered my spiritual gift of teaching. So God, in His kindness, helped me face my fear, and I slowly acquired the ability to speak in front of people—first in small Bible studies, then in larger classes, and finally to congregations. As I continued to speak, I not only became less fearful, but I also acquired the skills to speak effectively.

These illustrations of my natural and acquired abilities provide just a few examples of how exploring your personal makeup can lead to greater discernment of your calling.

Another useful hint I learned while exploring destiny was to look back through my life to see specific experiences God placed in my path that shaped my destiny. This exercise proved to me that God had actively been engaged throughout my life, even when I didn't recognize it. Certainly, my decision to go into nursing was one such destiny moment, for it was born out of my heart's desire to be used to save and heal others. The expression was off, but the destiny call was God-given.

Another example of a destiny moment occurred when I was on a bike ride minding my own business. It was a lovely Vineyard day, and I was enjoying spending time with my husband, brother, and sister-in-law.

As I pedaled away, the Lord interrupted my thoughts: "You like being in the back, don't you? It's a lot safer back there. You can guide and set the pace from the back without the risk of leading. This is not where I've called you to be. I've called you to be in the front."

Wow! "The truth hurts" was certainly true that day. In that moment, I knew God was right and was calling me to leadership. He had designed me to be a leader, no longer clinging to the safety of being behind others. God spoke into my destiny that day and powerfully altered it. It was a true destiny moment that changed the course of my life.

Understanding our wiring and God's divine touch throughout our lives can be useful pointers to our purpose.

Understanding our wiring and God's divine touch throughout our lives can be useful pointers to our purpose.

Another thing I discovered as I allowed the Lord to restore my heart was that looking back at the lies the Enemy planted can also give clues to your destiny. Do you remember how my voice was silenced and I was terrified into not speaking the truth? The Enemy had attacked me in the very arena in which God had designed for me to function: teaching and speaking His truth publicly. It is incredible to think how crafty and deceptive the Enemy is.

Another glaring example is how God had called me to minister to people, yet because of the lies the Enemy created about self-worth, I was terrified of people and felt safer going unnoticed—the very antithesis of God's call for me to lead.

I can't thank God enough for the way in which He has led me along the journey to a restored, resurrected heart that more fully expresses

Him, walks in true identity, and discovers more accurately the destiny of good works in Christ He has prepared in advance (Ephesians 2:10).

Confronting
the Darkness

For we do not wrestle against flesh and blood,
but against the rulers, against the authorities,
against the cosmic powers over this present darkness,
against the spiritual forces of evil in the heavenly places.
Ephesians 6:12

Can I be honest for a minute? Actually, that's laughable. Since when have I not been honest? I have been blatantly honest, so I won't stop now.

I hate having an enemy! From my earliest memories, I have always been a peacemaker. I was always watching everyone diligently to be sure all was well, ready to step in and intercept issues before they got uncomfortable, or smoothing ruffled feathers to restore peace. I hate battles, too, except the ones in movies where the good guys are assured victory.

After all the battling we've waged for wholeness and restoration in Christ, wouldn't it be nice if the Enemy would recede like a horrible nightmare and leave us alone? Unfortunately, that is not reality, and reality, being harsh at times, tells us we will be engaged in battle either until Christ returns or we die and go to heaven. Therefore, in order to be fully victorious, we will have to continually confront darkness as the divine battle heats up and roars louder.

For us to ultimately take a victory lap with Christ, we'll have to suit up in our divine armor, face our foe, trust our mighty warrior, and pray with persistence until the end.

Unlike my past tendency, we cannot afford to be passive or to mercifully give up territory and allow our opponent victory. The stakes are too high for us. In order for us to ultimately take a victory lap with Christ, we will have to suit up in our divine armor, face our foe, trust our Mighty Warrior, and pray with persistence until the end. Our victory over evil, destructive spiritual forces will then be assured. In the end, our success will bring glory to God.

Like I said at the start, I hate the Enemy and I hate being a part of a battle. Nevertheless, I made my choice long ago to follow Jesus, my Commander in Chief, and battle I will!

The Mighty Warrior

Admittedly, I can't say I feel strong enough to fight this cosmic battle. I do, though, love to watch the battles fought in the movie *Star Wars*, and I long to fight valiantly as the rebel forces did. I never realized that I would be called upon to fight as they did. The thought of it exhausts me!

But just when I start to feel freaked out and defeated, I'm reminded that I am not battling alone. Thankfully, God's Word reassures us that the battle is not ours, but God's (2 Chronicles 20:15), and it proceeds to provide dynamic examples of those who trusted God's promise while He proved faithful and willing to do battle for them.

It's easy to forget this reality in the heat of battle. Circumstances scream loudly, causing us to lose sight of God's ability to fight on our behalf. However, King David, who was well acquainted with fighting, promises us that God is strong and mighty in battle (Psalm 24:8). He should know! He is the one who took on Goliath with a slingshot after the whole Israelite army quaked in their boots. David slung the stone, but God enabled it to hit the bulls-eye, rendering Goliath, despite all his bravado, a defeated foe.

David, through this and many other battles, had firsthand knowledge of God the warrior. His stories recorded in the Bible underscore the miraculous ways God enabled David and the Israelites to rout their enemies.

David wasn't the only example whose experiences confirmed that God is mighty. The book of Exodus portrays God taking on powerful Egypt. The tale of God bringing the Israelites out of Egyptian bondage was miraculous from start to finish. He revealed Himself as a mighty warrior to the Israelites and also to Pharaoh and all of Egypt. God's impressive strength was revealed not only with the plagues the Egyptians suffered, but also when He enabled the Israelites to elude their enemy while literally walking out of Egypt through parted waters.

Can you imagine standing on the banks of the Red Sea and watching it part while a million people pass through—then witnessing the water come crashing back down, destroying Egypt's finest warriors? Talk about a mighty God!

Of course, the story of Gideon also shouts the mightiness of God. Gideon, the weak one with a false identity, was later used by God in miraculous ways to destroy Israel's enemy. The book of Judges retells Gideon's story, wherein we see God guiding Gideon to winnow the Israelite army down from twenty-two thousand warriors to a mere three hundred, seriously diminishing the odds of victory. However, God knew what He was doing, and through these three hundred faithful men, He brought a stunning defeat against the Midianites (Judges 7).

God proved Himself in battle back then, and He continues to prove Himself today. As we trust Him, follow His lead, and confront the enemy, He will surely bring victory to the battles we wage as we follow Him.

The Battle Continues, So "Suit Up"

We are encouraged in Ephesians 6:10 to "be strong in the Lord and in the strength of his might." The knowledge of His might and strength enables us to be strong. We realize that in our strength we can do nothing, but in His strength we can do everything.

Despite the battle being God's, He requires us to fight with Him. As any warrior knows, it is necessary to go into battle adequately outfitted with battle gear. David did not face Goliath without a weapon in his hand that God could use to

Despite the battle being God's, He requires us to fight with Him.

bring victory. Our divine battle will require no less suiting up. The apostle Paul encourages us to put on the whole armor of God, which enables us to stand against our enemy (Ephesians 6:11).

Unfortunately, God's saints don't always fully understand the battle they are in, and they often neglect to put on the armor that God has supplied for their protection and ongoing success. I was one who did not put on the armor of God. I had heard about the armor of God, but I didn't comprehend the armor's importance or the ongoing fight I was unknowingly engaged in. With maturity in Christ and the Word, I now understand and recognize the raging unseen, but very real, ongoing divine battle.

Sadly, some people mistakenly think this battle is against people. It is easy to feel that way when others don't treat us right, when they make us mad, or when they betray, abuse, reject, or in some way harm us. Consequently, we then put up our fists, raise our voice, seek revenge, or display some other reaction in order to get back at our imagined foe.

People are not our enemies. However, the Bible tells us vehemently that we are not battling against people. People are not our enemies. Sometimes it is hard to comprehend this, but it's true. Our battle is not against people but against evil spiritual forces (Ephesians 6:12).

With this in mind, in order to be victorious against our real enemy, we must put on appropriate gear that is specific to spiritual battles. This armor, as the Bible calls it, will help us to withstand and effectively battle the Enemy.

What is this armor? Take a peek and see how Ephesians 6:14–17 refers to this spiritual armor:

- *Belt of truth*: Our lifelong journey is about pursuing the truth and getting rid of lies. Since we have expended a lot of energy getting rid of the deceptive strongholds of the Enemy, it is critical for us to keep the truth tightly fastened and encircling us so that deceit will no longer have its way in our lives.

- *Breastplate of righteousness*: Christ made us righteous through redemption. This righteousness protects our hearts from being drawn into the temptations Satan tries to lure us into. Setting our hearts on daily obedience to Christ and God's Word will protect us from veering unintentionally into the landmines our unrighteous enemy has set to trip us up and harm us.

- *Feet shod with the gospel of peace*: Our lives must be firmly planted on the good news of the gospel. We must always be ready to share the peace available to all through the gospel. Many people are not gifted evangelists, but our lives intersect daily with people who don't know the freedom and message of reconciliation found in the gospel. As we follow the leading of the Holy Spirit, He will give us eyes to see those with whom we are to interact and encourage with the truth and peace of the gospel.

- *Shield of faith*: A warrior's shield protects and shields him from the attack of the enemy's weaponry. Our faith, acting as a shield, extinguishes the lies that the enemy hurls to wound and take us out. Faith even as small as a mustard seed is capable of moving mountains (Matthew 17:20). Holding our faith up against the Enemy will successfully defeat any fiery darts he sends our way.

- *Helmet of salvation*: The battlefield with Satan is primarily in our minds. The helmet of salvation fits securely on our head to protect it, and it rests upon the finished work of Christ, ensuring our eternity. Salvation, both eternal and ongoing sanctification, secures us against all spiritual arguments the Enemy throws to destroy our rightful inheritance as saints.

- *Sword of the Spirit*: The Word of God is a mighty offensive weapon we can wield to strike down the Enemy and his lies. Christ modeled this offensive assault, declaring the Word of God when Satan threw temptations at Him in the wilderness (Luke 4:1–13). We, too, can declare the Word of God over our specific situations to offensively battle the Enemy's schemes.

Our armor is not like any typical armor that has been used throughout history. It is, nonetheless, effectively engineered to exert the maximum amount of damage to our corporate enemy and his minions. If we want to successfully be "the head and not the tail," as God intends us to be (Deuteronomy 28:13), then we must obey Scripture and put on the whole armor of God. A piece applied here and there will not result in the triumphant overcoming that the Lord painfully secured for us.

For those who might find it helpful, I have included a daily prayer at the end of the chapter that will help you effectively suit up, as God encourages you to do.

Authority Is Ours—Use It!

In our quest to take back the territory of our lives with the weapons Christ has provided for us, one undeniable truth the Enemy tries to keep secret is that Christ has given us all authority and power over the Enemy. When Christ died and shed His blood for our sins, He took back the authority, which Satan assumed over Adam and Eve when they succumbed to his deceit and their relationship with God was fractured. Christ turned around and gave this authority back to His disciples, securing their victory over Satan (Genesis 3; Ephesians 1; Colossians 2:13–15; Hebrews 2:14–15).

Jesus promised, "Behold, I have given you authority to tread on serpents and scorpions, and over all the power of the enemy, and nothing shall hurt you" (Luke 10:19). This is amazing! We have authority and all power over the Enemy! This is good news to those who are captive. We don't have to stay in the clutches of the Enemy. Christ's sacrifice guaranteed it.

Consider with me for a minute what this really means. We have authority and all power. I love how simplistically the authors of the *Freedom Class Manual* describe these terms: "Authority is the right to rule, and power is the ability to rule."[36] In other words, we have authority because God gave us a new position as a result of our redemption. This position, seated with Christ (Ephesians 2:6) as adopted sons and daughters, gives us the authority to rule over the Enemy as well as the power or ability to rule.

I don't know about you, but I don't always *feel* able to rule. The point is that it's not about how one feels. Our ability to rule is a reality whether we feel able or not. It's about what Christ did and then delegated to us.

Too often we focus on ourselves, forgetting about God. God doesn't expect us to rule in our own strength. He is the Mighty Warrior who backs up His Word and provides the Holy Spirit, giving us the power and the ability to rule. Acts 1:8 confirms this truth: "You will receive power when the Holy Spirit has come upon you, and you will be my witnesses in Jerusalem and in all Judea and Samaria, and to the end of the earth."

When I compare the disciples before and after they were filled with the Holy Spirit, I see a world of difference. They were changed from children in the faith to men who ruled with authority while manifesting the kingdom of God. Spanning the time of the infilling of the Holy Spirit in Acts throughout the New Testament to Revelation, we see countless examples of Christ's disciples using their authority and power over the Enemy with miraculous results.

Unfortunately, it appears that many Christians today are not walking in authority and power. For them, the revelation seems to be elusive. After years as a Christian, I feel as if I'm only scratching the surface of understanding the authority I've been given. I know the position Christ has obtained for us, yet the full revelation has taken longer to sink in.

In our modern times, it is often difficult for us to understand the concept of ruling and reigning. We are far removed from political systems that use this form of authority. However, the truth remains that we are called to rule and reign with Christ (2 Timothy 2:12; Revelation 5:9–10). Not only are we called to reign in Christ's future kingdom, but we are also called to walk in the authority and power Christ gave to us so we could rule and reign against the kingdom of darkness now.

As warriors, we are called by Christ to continually protect the jurisdiction of our hearts and that of others whose hearts He has reclaimed. This prohibits the Enemy from regaining and taking back territory that Christ has set free. Christ has given us everything we will ever need to successfully walk in authority and to powerfully rule with Him in His kingdom on earth and in the kingdom to come. He has given us both the weapons

> Christ has given us everything we'll ever need to successfully walk in authority and powerfully rule with Him.

and the armor. Now is the time for us to step up into the position Christ has secured for us as kings and priests who are ready to rule and reign.

If something is standing in the way of you fully engaging in your rightful place with Christ, ask the Lord to reveal what is hindering you. Then ask Him to remove the obstacles. Walking with Christ as royalty in full authority is at the heart of God's plan for your life.

Facing Your Foe

Facing a foe as a peacemaker is not something I ever wanted to do. Conflict might just as well have been a four-letter word to me. I used to do everything in my power to avoid having a foe. I would sidestep even a whiff of anything that resembled conflict. Aside from my parents' tumultuous relationship, my concept of conflict and battles was shaped by boring historical facts from television and movies. They all seemed far removed and unconnected to my everyday life. Still, I was always inspired by the stories that highlighted courageous acts by heroes against their enemy.

As I watched these heroes, I would wonder what enabled them to face their foes with such courage. What motivated them to run into battle with determination, never backing down, and persisting until they were assured victory, or died trying? I concluded early on that only a handful of people were created with the special traits required for these courageous feats. In light of my history, I figured I was definitely missing this special trait.

Thinking about the well-known battle of David and Goliath, it would be easy to self-righteously proclaim, "I would stand up like David!" Honestly, though, I know I would more likely be like the soldiers of the Israelite army who were terrorized by their enemy.

Imagine my surprise—no, my sheer horror—when I learned that I, too, am in a battle. At that time, I was scared to death of Satan. In my mind, he was the embodiment of the man who had abused me. I was convinced that Satan would destroy me. Thankfully, more than forty years later, I can heartily testify that the Lord helped me stand, wage war, and defeat the foe—a far cry from being destroyed. I learned that victory over the Enemy has nothing to do with special traits endowed to a few chosen individuals. Actually, God has given every individual what they need to oppose the Enemy and overcome in battle.

As children of God, we all have what it takes to be heroes. God made sure of it when He gave His Son to die for our sins. He provides what we need, and He enables

> As children of God, we all have what it takes to be a hero.

and sanctifies us so we can be victorious warriors in the divine battles.

Along with the things that heroes of the faith use and that we have already discussed (weaponry, armor, trust in God, and standing firm), I've noticed several other qualities that propel individuals to victory. The battle account of David and Goliath serves to highlight several of these qualities (1 Samuel 17:8–51).

The Bible paints a picture of David not measuring up to man's standards of being a hero—not having any special traits that would mark him as one. However, David was well-known to God, and God saw things in David that no one else saw. Throughout the years, God successfully developed David to be His chosen warrior because of these unseen characteristics. God desires to develop these same qualities in us as well, building us into mighty warriors who faithfully serve Him.

The first quality highlighted by this narrative is that David knew and had confidence in God. As a Jewish boy and as a shepherd, David, through his education and experience, obtained a genuine understanding of God's character. The Greek word in the New Testament transliterated as *ginosko* sheds light on the revelation and intimate knowledge David had about God, and that God wants us to have about Him. This word refers to an intimate knowledge we have when we are fully acquainted with something. It points to the closeness a husband and wife share during sexual intimacy. David had this same deep experiential *ginosko* knowledge of God, and he trusted God's love and ability to war on his behalf.

I can now understand why, when I was a young Christian who had little knowledge of God's character, my fear of Satan made him seem glaringly more powerful to me. I tasted firsthand the damage and injustice the Enemy had wreaked on me, leaving me weak and unable to fight like David did.

However, as I grew in intimate knowledge of God's character through study and personal experience, my confidence and trust developed to the point where I was willing to battle one of the Goliaths in my life: fear.

This enemy was no less intimidating. My enemy of fear screamed threats into my ear to keep me bound in inactivity, just as Goliath did to the Israelite army. Like those soldiers, I was at the mercy of my fear. As I grew in the knowledge of God and His love for me, I confidently learned to face my foe, just as David did.

Another necessary quality David exhibited was courage. David's foundation of understanding God's character engendered courage, and that courage led to action in the face of fear. David knew God, but it could have stopped there with Goliath perpetually intimidating the Israelite army. However, David's knowledge of God gave him the courage to be willing to defend His reputation, so he courageously stepped forward with his slingshot. David's courage in facing such a formidable foe is incredible to me and leaves me wondering how he could do it.

"I learned that courage was not the absence of fear, but the triumph over it."[37] Those words from Nelson Mandela illuminated an important truth to me: courage did not represent a lack of fear but a determination not to let fear stop you from action.

I once thought that heroes who charged courageously into battle never wrestled with fear the way I did. What I've since learned is that these great men and women refused to listen to their fears, but faced their foes in spite of it.

> No matter the size of the battle, each gives opportunity for us to stand up courageously against our foe.

We may never be in a physical battle like David, Gideon, or those who fight for our country. Nevertheless, we are faced daily with the opportunity to fight our personal battles—some big and some little. No matter the size of the battle, each gives us the opportunity to stand up courageously against our foe. Having a mindset like this opens the way for God to do mighty things.

A third quality revealed in David's story is a passion for God's cause. David's passion for God's cause created an indignation in him: how dare anyone challenge God and His army!

Throughout history, people's passion for their causes has enabled them to battle zealously. A glaring example of this is Martin Luther King Jr. He held a strong conviction of a righteous cause, and this enabled him to face unbelievably difficult circumstances. In the end, he gave his life battling for that cause. The battle he passionately fought continues to have long-lasting consequences for the equality our country values today.

Companies that push their abundance of causes today recognize that passion for a cause is powerful. Their advertising campaigns attempt to incite an individual's passion that brings about involvement. They are well aware of the value of passion for their endeavors.

As I serve God and become increasingly aware of His mission, I find my passion ignited for His causes. Seeing these causes revealed in Isaiah 61, and fulfilled in Christ as recorded in Luke 4, I have become passionate to be used for these same causes, such as bringing the good news and setting captives free. Passion to see these verses materialize in people's lives has become a driving force in my life. This passion enables me to zealously battle the foes who are set against the purpose and mission of God.

The last quality I will mention is that of persistence in securing victory. This was not necessarily required of David's fight against Goliath, but it is no less crucial. Some battles are more like quick clashes. Others may take years to successfully win. Still others may not be won this side of heaven. Nonetheless, with the Holy Spirit working through us, we have everything we need to persist and succeed. The Holy Spirit is able to supply power to our situation, infusing us with His strength when we are at our weakest (2 Corinthians 12:9–10). It may not have taken David long to take down Goliath, but David's future battles required him to persist, even when he was at his weakest and the odds were against him.

Facing our personal enemies and securing lasting victory will also require unrelenting resistance. I have experienced several areas of deep captivity. These have required me to fight the same persistent battle and apply extra vigilance while the enemy attempts to lure me back into captivity from freedom.

One of these deep areas is rejection, which entered my life when I was a baby. God has uncovered the lies I believed and has brought great healing and freedom to me. However, because this stronghold was so deeply rooted with many convoluted layers, I have had to persistently face this spirit and resist its attempt to reclaim territory in my heart. God promises, "Resist the devil, and he will flee from you" (James 4:7). I have found this to be true in my life, and I know that the Holy Spirit will battle with you and make it true in your life if you also faithfully resist Satan.

God is quite adept at taking ordinary men and women and developing them into mighty warriors.

Although we may not see ourselves as heroes, God is quite adept at taking ordinary men and women, such as Gideon and Esther, and developing them into mighty warriors who do great exploits against the enemy. We all have what it takes to be heroes and to be great in the kingdom, standing up courageously while resisting Satan until he falls defeated.

God's mission on earth is to infiltrate the frontiers of enemy occupation and recapture territory, whether in hearts, people, or nations. God chooses to do this through the lives of ordinary people like you and me, whom He trains for battle. God has done it before in others, and He can surely do it again in you.

The Place of Prayer

The place of prayer in confronting the Enemy can't be stated enough. It is the critical connection we need with our Commander in Chief.

As anyone versed in warfare strategy knows, one successful strategy is to cut off your opponent's communication lines. Without the ability to communicate with your teammates, you are isolated and vulnerable to enemy attack. Therefore, maintaining prayer (our communication line to God) is important for enemy defeat.

Prayer's impact is too often minimized because it is misunderstood. As a young Christian, I learned the ACTS formula for prayer. I thought I was praying if I followed it verbatim: Adoration, Confession, Thanksgiving, and Supplication. For me, prayer was about following the formula.

The ACTS prayer model certainly contains important elements of prayer, but what I didn't understand was that the fundamental essence of prayer is intimacy. My rote prayers of strictly following the ACTS model were not breeding intimacy with God. Natural ways of building intimacy with people include spending time together, listening, speaking, sharing, and enjoying one another's company. Similarly, developing intimacy with God in prayer includes availability, listening, waiting in stillness, reading God's Word, and interacting with Him.

The place of intimacy with God is exactly the place the Enemy tries to attack, thus hoping to block communication lines between God and His children. For a lot of people, myself included, intimacy proves challenging and leaves a person feeling vulnerable and unsafe.

I remember when God first spoke to me about intimacy with Him. Having been sexually abused, intimacy was threatening and difficult for me. When God impressed me to study the Song of Solomon, I emotionally put on my track shoes, knowing it was about intimacy.

About a month later, I started feeling the absence of God's presence. Calling out to Him, I asked, *Where have You gone, Lord?*

His simple reply was, "Where have *you* gone?"

In that moment, I recognized my deep wound of intimacy. I also realized that "real warfare in the kingdom of God is always concerned with the battle for intimacy."[38] Satan had successfully, albeit briefly, attacked my communication line—intimacy—with God.

The Enemy is well aware that a believer's intimacy with God is critical, for it is the place of power, strength, healing, authority, and freedom from captivity for believers, as well as wisdom and revelation into Satan's playbook. When we are separated from our connection with the Lord, Satan knows we are in the dark and are vulnerable to his schemes and attack.

The Enemy is well aware that a believer's intimacy with God is critical.

Many believers confirm that the reconnaissance received from the Holy Spirit provided valuable insight into their situation. I've experienced this often. One such time, I was feeling down and discouraged, seemingly for no reason. While in prayer, the Holy Spirit impressed upon me that my feelings were revealing what our church congregation felt and that it was a spiritual attack. This divine insight enabled me to pray specifically for the church. Intimacy in prayer that day proved valuable in confronting the Enemy.

Sadly, listening to the body of Christ, it seems as if the Enemy's strategy for battling intimacy with God is proving effective, keeping us so busy and distracted that we lose sight of the importance of our life-giving prayer link with God.

Even though I understand how critical intimacy is, I've fallen prey to overwhelming responsibilities, and at times I have allowed prayer to fall to the bottom of my priority list. With everything else seeming to be more pressing, prayer was reduced to quickly making requests as I rushed through the day. I always wonder how I could be so deceived at those times as to think that anything is more important than my relationship with the Lord. How does that happen? It is an enemy attack!

Another, more subtle, attack that keeps us busy and away from intimacy is the deception to do things for the Lord rather than to be with the Lord. Years ago, when I was a young mother and Sunday school coordinator, the Lord impressed me to step down from ministry, as He wanted to teach me to *be* and not just to *do*. At the time, I had no idea what He meant, but I obeyed. That was when I started learning about intimacy and being with Him. I have heard people say (and I agree) that God created us to be human beings, not human doings. How easy it is to forget this and to forget that God intends our *doing* to overflow from our *being* with Him.

The momentum of life in the United States is on overdrive, and it's easy to be swept along.

Even after so many years, if I'm not careful, I still struggle to prioritize my time with God. The momentum of life in the United States is on overdrive, and it's easy to be swept along unknowingly by the Enemy's efficacious ploy to keep us so busy that we lose sight of how far we have drifted from intimacy with God. It's no wonder that in these times we feel like we're walking through a spiritual desert without a sense of God's presence, feeling weak and vulnerable to Satan's attacks.

Many people express how their busyness actually necessitates more prayer. Martin Luther revealed this reality in the busyness of his life when he said (paraphrased), "I have so much to do today that I'm going to need to spend three hours in prayer in order to be able to get it all done."[39] I'm not at the place where I have devoted three hours to prayer yet, but Luther's statement challenges me to take a hard look at myself and evaluate if I'm prioritizing intimacy with God or allowing myself to slack off.

The importance of prayer relayed in Scripture is not a suggestion but an expectation. It is something literally spoken about hundreds of times in the Bible. The disciples assumed that everyone prayed. Jesus, as told in the Gospels, modeled the importance of prayer by frequently escaping to solitary places where He communed with the Father. We are told that Christ did only what the Father willed (John 5:30). How did He know what the Father wanted Him to do? He learned His Father's will in the place of intimate prayer. How did He know how to battle the Enemy? He learned this in the place of intimate prayer. If our Lord found it desirable and necessary to be alone with the Father, I can only imagine how much more we need to do the same.

Our success and victory over Satan might require making radical adjustments in our lives if we are to take our rightful place and be the mighty warriors God intends for us to be. We each have the potential and the legal right. In order to be successful, though, we need to remain tethered to our Commander in Chief. After all, He has already secured our victory.

> **To be successful, we need to remain tethered to our Commander in Chief.**

The following prayer examples are ways you can suit up and prepare for battle[40] or secure protection over your life or the lives of others.[41]

Simple Prayer for Putting on the Whole Armor of God

Dear God, today we put on the full armor to guard our lives against attack. We put on the belt of truth to protect against lies and deception. We put on the breastplate of righteousness to protect our hearts from the temptations we battle. We put the gospel of peace on our feet so that we're ready to take Your light wherever You send us this day. We choose to walk in the peace and freedom of Your Spirit and not be overcome with fear and anxious thoughts. We take up Your shield of faith that will extinguish all the darts and threats hurled our way by the Enemy. We believe in Your power to protect us, and we choose to trust in You. We put on the helmet of salvation, which covers our minds and thoughts, reminding us that we are children of the day, forgiven, set free, and saved by the grace of Christ Jesus. We take up the sword of the Spirit, your very Word, the one offensive weapon given to us for battle, which has the power to demolish strongholds. It is alive, active, and sharper than any double-edged sword.

We ask for Your help in remembering to put on Your full armor every day, for You give us all that we need to stand firm in this world. Forgive us, God, for the times we've been unprepared or too busy to care, or when we have tried to fight and wrestle in our own strength.

Thank You that we never fight alone, for You are constantly at work on our behalf shielding, protecting, strengthening, exposing deeds of darkness, bringing to light what needs to be known, and covering us from the cruel attacks we face, even when we're unaware. In the powerful name of Jesus, Amen.

Prayer of Psalm 91 for Protection

Thank You, Father, that I dwell in the shelter of the Most High and abide in the shadow of the Almighty. I will say to the Lord, "My refuge and my fortress, my God, in whom I trust."

For You will deliver me from the snare of the fowler and from the deadly pestilence. You will cover me with Your pinions, and under Your wings I will find refuge. Your faithfulness is a shield and buckler. I will not fear the terror of the night, nor the arrow that flies by day, nor the pestilence that stalks in darkness, nor the destruction that wastes at noonday.

A thousand may fall at my side, ten thousand at my right hand, but it will not come near me. I will only look with my eyes and see the recompense of the wicked.

Because I have made the Lord my dwelling place—the Most High, who is my refuge—no evil shall be allowed to befall me, no plague come near my tent.

For You will command Your angels concerning me to guard me in all my ways. On their hands they will bear me up, lest I strike my foot against a stone. I will tread on the lion and the adder; the young lion and the serpent I will trample underfoot.

Because I hold fast to You in love, You will deliver me. You will protect me because I know Your name. When I call to You, You will answer me; You will be with me in trouble; You will rescue me and honor me. With long life You will satisfy me and show me Your salvation.

Living above the Ashes

*His divine power has granted to us all things that
pertain to life and godliness, through the knowledge
of him who called us to his own glory and excellence,
by which he has granted to us his precious and
very great promises, so that through them you may
become partakers of the divine nature,
having escaped from the corruption that
is in the world because of sinful desire.*
2 Peter 1:3-4

ow! What a journey we've been on! It would be easy to stop
here and become comfortable with what the Lord has done, yet
it would be short of our goal of recapturing the destiny and purpose God has for us.

It's easy to lose heart just before the final push to cross the finish line.
Any woman who has gone through the last stage of labor when delivering a baby can probably remember the same feeling of wanting to give up
and finish later. However, accomplishing a difficult and laborious task—
whether a birth, a marathon, or a challenging project—is exhilarating
and deeply fulfilling. Therefore, I want to encourage you to press into
your destiny so you can say in the end with Paul, "I have fought the good
fight, I have finished the race, I have kept the faith" (2 Timothy 4:7).

Why is this so important? It is important so that you, too, can receive the crown of righteousness (2 Timothy 4:8) and hear those prized words from your Savior, "Well done, good and faithful servant" (Matthew 25:21).

As you have seen, getting to the finish line is not always easy. It requires faith, perseverance, determination, and suffering. *Yet that crown and those words from Jesus will make the journey well worth it.* Christ doesn't intend for our lives to be miserable as we finish our race. The passage from 2 Peter at the beginning of this chapter highlights this and promises us more than suffering and misery. It promises all things that pertain to life and godliness through the knowledge of Him who has called us to His own glory and excellence, by which He has granted to us His precious and very great promises, so that through them we may partake of His divine nature. Besides the crown, this is exactly what I'm pressing on for. The promises in the Bible are as true for us today as they were for the early Christians when the words were first penned.

As I was contemplating this chapter, the Holy Spirit reminded me of an experience I had when my journey was beginning. I was at the weeklong counseling retreat learning about dysfunction and woundedness. Using an object lesson to prove their point, the counselors covered their model with a sheet that represented dysfunction. They pulled the sheet down to the person's waist, proclaiming that this was as free as any of us participants could ever be.

They explained that as we continued to pursue healing, our children could experience more freedom as they consciously pursued healing as well. This was represented when the sheet was pulled down to knee level. The meaning was clear: as each successive generation sought freedom, they would progressively become more healed and freer from dysfunction.

You might wonder why I would include this discouraging story. I'll tell you why: I included it because it is a lie! Yes, it is a lie. If this illustration were true, then all the Bible promises would be false. The promises are either true or not. They are either "yes" and "Amen" or they aren't (2 Corinthians 1:20).

I have experienced the truth of God's promises and am a living testimony to them. We can be set free in our lifetime. If the promises are true for me, I can assure you they are true for you too. Christ has set us free, and Paul encourages us to stand firm and not submit again to a yoke of slavery (Galatians 5:1).

I refuse to have a metaphorical sheet wrapped around my legs. I refuse to go back to a life of lies, and I am pressing on to experience all of God's promises. Simply stated, this is the essence of living above the ashes, of no longer living in slavery to the Enemy and his lies, but instead tenaciously chasing after the promise to be a partaker of the divine nature of Christ and fulfill His purpose for us.

The journey is not always easy; it can be downright discouraging. Most of the time, however, it's exhilarating. A life above the ashes necessitates continual effort that includes moving on from our past, embracing our rewritten history, actively reclaiming our destiny, remembering that God is in control and has a plan for us, and pursuing a righteous life.

A life above the ashes necessitates continual effort.

Although I haven't reached the end of the road (the road doesn't end until we reach heaven), I can promise you that a life above the ashes—a life of freedom, meaning, abundance, gratitude, change, and purpose—is possible now.

It is so worth it! If I can live above the ashes, you can too.

Rewritten History

Embracing a life that is above the ashes requires a willingness to let go of the old and receive God's rewriting of our history. The challenge of going back and exploring our background is that we may get stuck there and not move forward into what God has for us. We may find it easier to cling to the familiarity of brokenness, to be unwilling to allow our perspective to change, or to lack willingness to put the effort into becoming free.

Of course, this is a danger. Nonetheless, we can trust the One who has started this journey in us and can confidently know that He will lovingly and encouragingly assist us as we move forward.

When I think of having a new history, my mind drifts back to the day I was adopted by Dad. The judge's simple signature changed me from a *Stephens*, with its associated identity and inheritance, to a *Keeler* with a separate identity and inheritance. For better or worse, my life was indelibly marked by the stroke of a pen; I was no longer able to cling to what I had known since birth. This new identity, which unfolded over the years, proved more damaging than live-giving to my vulnerable soul.

Similar to a physical adoption, there is a spiritual adoption we experience that occurs the moment we receive Christ as our Savior. In a moment, with the spiritual transaction of confession and a divine signature, you receive a new name, identity, and inheritance. You instantaneously become a child of God with a new family and a new name: *in Christ*. You are no longer bound by your history on earth. You have a new history that is rewritten over your past history.

For you hopeless romantics or those who are visually inclined like I am, I find that the fairy tale of Cinderella lends a powerful illustration to the truth of our shifting new identity and inheritance. Here are some of the most obvious similarities:

- Servitude to the wicked stepmother and sisters resembles our servitude to Satan and his forces.

- Cinderella's own attempts to make herself worthy to be a part of the celebration resembles the attempts we make to create lives that are worthy.

- Cinderella's transformation at the hands of the fairy godmother resembles our complete transformation when we receive Christ's redemption.

- All of the maidens' attempts to have their feet fit into the glass slipper was to no avail. These efforts remind us that the only way to transformation is through accepting Christ. Self-efforts cannot achieve the promise.

- Cinderella's life changed in an instant from servitude to royalty, and all the benefits of the position were immediately available to her. This resembles our instant change of position from servitude to divine royalty, along with all of the God-given benefits inherent in His adoption of us that are immediately made available to us.

The symbolism of this story puts flesh on truths that are often difficult to comprehend, and this symbolism resonates deeply in my heart. More importantly, the Bible confirms this truth of our new position. Paul declares it often, but he made it crystal clear when he penned, "So you are no longer a slave, but a son, and if a son, then an heir through God" (Galatians 4:7).

Do we realize how incredible this change is? We become a child of God and heir to all He has! We become royalty and sit with the King of kings as heir to all He has! The enormity of this is unfathomable. Do you find this truth as difficult to grasp as I do?

I remember how long it took me to get used to my new name, identity, and inheritance after I first married my husband. Similarly, walking in our new divine royal robes and history will take time.

Surprisingly, people sometimes think that this new position with a re-written history will mean that everything in our painful past is obliterated and all scars are removed. I'm sorry to disappoint you, but this is not at all true. If this were true, then why did Jesus still have scars after His resurrection? We know that the scars on His hands, feet, and side remained. We also know they weren't painful and did not affect His life. The pain inflicted by the wounds that resulted in His scars was gone and no longer imposed suffering. Likewise, our scars will remain. Yet once our wounds are healed and the resulting infections are cauterized and removed, the scars that remain no longer hold any pain. Thus, the scars give evidence of what once was. What is interesting about our scars is that the Lord uses them to reveal truth to others—truth of who He is and what He is capable of.

We see Jesus doing this very thing in the case of "doubting Thomas." Thomas said that he wouldn't believe that Jesus was resurrected until he saw the scars. When the Lord held out His hand and revealed His scars to Thomas, Thomas saw the truth and believed (John 20:24–29). Our scars also have this capability. They can help others see the resurrection power of God that is displayed through our healed heart wounds. I love this! My wounds are recycled by God to bring healing to others. Beauty is reconstructed from my ashes (Isaiah 61:3). Only God can take the ashes of our lives and build an amazing purpose out of them. This is His promise to me, and this is His promise to you.

Surrendering our lives to God and letting go of the broken foundations of our past history allows God to give us a new history.

Surrendering our lives to God and letting go of the broken foundations of our past history allows God to give us a new history. This brings abundance not only to our own lives, but also to the lives of others. God desires to reshape and re-align our lives with His original intent and purpose so we fulfill His mission.

My prayer is that you will learn from and let go of the painful parts of your history, and that you will hold on to the good and embrace the new history God has for you. In doing so, you will be taking another step toward reclaiming your destiny and fulfilling God's plan for your life.

God's Got a Plan

Do you realize that God has a plan for your life? It is a plan that dates back to before you were born (Psalm 139:16). Your days and purpose were seen in the heart of God when you were only a thought in His mind. He is committed to seeing you fulfill that purpose.

It is difficult to wrap our minds around this fact because we often envision God as an overbearing dictator who is telling us what to do and how to do it. That is not at all true. God has lovingly and uniquely crafted us for the specific way He is calling us to impact our world. He has a vision for our lives.

Thinking of God's vision for our lives, I can't help but think of Abraham and Sarah. Their story reveals that God has a plan for individual lives that far exceeds any plan we can envision. Abraham and Sarah planned to have a child and live like everyone else. There was one small hitch in their plan—they were barren. Regardless, God's purpose and plan for their lives was much grander, for it included making Abraham a great nation with offspring as numerous as the stars in the sky (Genesis 12:2; 15:5).

Like Abraham and Sarah, we often have personal plans that pale in comparison to the vision and plan God has for our lives. God often gives us glimmers of His vision, as He did with Abraham, to encourage us to believe and persevere. Frequently, it takes years to realize His plan and destiny. Abraham waited decades to see the fulfillment of God's promised vision. We might have to wait a while as well, but God has a vision for us, and He is entirely capable of bringing it to pass.

We are assured of God's faithfulness. I know from experience that waiting can be discouraging. Nonetheless, placing trust in God, in His plan, and in His faithfulness amid this discouragement can keep you secure, as it did for me.

Trusting and depending on God can also be challenging. It is so much easier to trust in things we see. I'm sure Abraham and Sarah found it difficult to trust when all they could see were their old bodies, which were getting older by the moment. Yet Hebrews 11 testifies that Abraham was known for his faith, and it confirms that in the midst of his longing, even with his failure in regard to Ishmael, he continued to trust and have faith. Thus, God miraculously fulfilled His promise to Abraham and Sarah, making them parents to Isaac and later of a great nation (Genesis 21:1–3).

When God gives us a vision for our destiny, it is easy to focus on ourselves and contradict Him, just as Abraham did (Genesis 17:17). Sadly, the contradiction boils down to our envisioning a purpose and plan that is devoid of God's divine power to fulfill it. This is the antithesis of God's plan. When He reveals His vision, it is always with His capabilities factored in. He knows we cannot do much that is of eternal substance on our own, but with God, all things are possible (Matthew 19:26).

As we lean into trusting God's plan and cease contradicting it with negative self-talk, we will see God lead us into fulfillment. My youngest brother, Ethan, is a gift-ed artist. I'll never forget a drawing he made when he was younger. It was a colorful picture that had the word "can't" written on it with a fist coming up and punching the "t" out of the word. I think of it often, and I use it as a reminder that God can turn all my "can'ts" into "cans." If you trust and depend on God, He can accomplish all He envisions for your life.

> As we lean into trusting God's plan, and cease contradicting it with negative self-talk, we will see God lead us into fulfillment.

Writing this book has been a great example of turning a "can't" into a "can." I told you that decades ago God encouraged me to write.

Immediately, I disqualified myself with the negative self-talk of "can't" due to my natural challenges. Over the years, I fretted, dreamed, and planned, but I felt as if I failed God miserably by not obeying Him.

This past spring, God maneuvered a divine setup to get me to write this book. I understood it as God's timing, and I knew that I could do it with the Holy Spirit's help. God is able to do all He purposes through us if we only believe.

Throughout the years of your journey, you may at times feel as if you are failing and are never going to accomplish anything that God has put in your heart. You might identify with the roller coaster I mentioned in chapter three—the ups and downs of trying and failing. I'm sure Abraham might have felt as if he had failed God when he took matters into his own hands and conceived Ishmael. At these times, it's easy to want to throw in the towel. Life isn't always easy, especially when we are weighed down with the perception of failure and have a condemning enemy nipping at our heels.

At times like these, we need to remember that failures provide opportunities to learn. John Maxwell wrote a book called *Failing Forward*.[42] I love this concept because it brings much hope in the midst of failure. In his book, Maxwell explains that we can expect to fail (it is inevitable), but it is important to keep going and use failure to thrust us forward with valuable lessons.

God can use everything, even our failures, to accomplish His will and purpose for our lives.

Therefore, please don't give up. Remember that with God, all things are possible. Abraham's failure, but continued faith, testify to this truth. God can use everything, even our failures, to accomplish His will and purpose for our lives.

Years ago, my husband experienced a seeming career failure, although we both now contend that it wasn't. Now I can see how God extracted us from a situation and relocated us to fulfill His purpose and our destiny. We now live on a beautiful complex with our son, his wife and children, and our daughter.

For years prior to this, the complex was in our hearts, but we had no idea how God would orchestrate it. The "failure" maneuvered us into position to be ready for God's plan—some of which we have fulfilled, and some that is yet to unfold. If God hadn't let circumstances play out in my husband's situation, we wouldn't be where we are today. In the face of seeming failure, we refused to be defined by failure; instead, we continued to trust God for our destiny, even when it looked impossible.

God was faithful to us. He will be faithful to you, too, as He works in your circumstances (failures included) to reclaim your destiny.

Reclaiming Your Destiny

From a very young age, there has been something deep inside me desiring to make a difference in the world. At first, I thought the difference was to touch others' lives as a nurse. However, as I began experiencing my rewritten history, I knew that reclaiming my destiny involved more than nursing alone.

During my years of intensive healing, I often thought the dream in my heart would never be fulfilled. Since then, though, I have learned that dreams don't originate in us. God places these dreams in our hearts.

The realization that dreams are God-given brought much freedom to me. I recognized then that He would make them come to pass. I would be responsible to follow God's leading and do what I could, but in the end, God was ultimately the One responsible to fulfill His dream in me.

Have you heard the saying, "I do what I can do, and God does what only He can"? This applies to fulfilling our God-given dreams and reclaiming our destiny. I can't just be a couch potato and expect God to deliver purpose and destiny to my doorstep in the same way that Amazon brings packages.

God never does the things we can do. He is more interested in helping us become spiritual-ly mature. You don't help individuals to mature by doing everything for them. Just think what would happen if parents didn't encourage or let their kids learn to walk, run, or feed themselves. At some point, parents expect their children to increase in maturity and become responsible.

God never does the things we can do.

God is no different with His children. He leads and teaches us, but He expects us to actively participate in the sanctification process.

God leads by His Word, by encouragement from a believer, or by a desire within. Part of discovering destiny is taking on the next thing God shows you to do; following step by step leads you closer to your destiny. You can't learn to run until you learn to walk. Similarly, God progressively brings us into destiny as we follow His steps to get there.

Understanding and then working in my ministerial purpose didn't just happen because God led me to Isaiah 61. I had to put a lot of effort into preparation as He led, including going back for my degree in Christian leadership, assisting ministries, volunteering in various positions at church, and engaging in hours upon hours of study. Every step of the way, God opened opportunities for me to accept or reject. As I faithfully and boldly pursued opportunities and put in the time and effort required, I acquired the wisdom, knowledge, and abilities necessary for me to fulfill God's call. Walking into destiny requires this preparation and following God's leading in taking the next step and accomplishing the next goal He places in front of you.

Reclaiming our destiny reminds me of doing a puzzle. I love doing puzzles, especially with my oldest son. He actually has the nickname "Puzzle boy" because he's so good at fitting things together.

The last time we did a puzzle together, we went for the challenging thousand-piece puzzle. My son, loving a challenge, informed me that we couldn't look at the reference picture to help fit it together. You've got to be kidding! Blind puzzling? Talk about challenging! However, it reminded me how often trying to find our purpose is like doing a puzzle—sometimes it feels as if we are doing it blindly. Nevertheless, just as puzzles have their edge pieces, colors, and shapes, so there are clues that assist us in putting our destiny together.

We have already discussed a few of these clues, such as destiny moments in our lives, talents, abilities, and natural and acquired skills. Nevertheless, I would be remiss not to mention passion. What are you passionate about? What makes you so exhilarated that you are like a light bulb that is burning at one hundred and fifty watts or more?

Telling or teaching people about the truth of God's character, ways, and mission does this for me. Sharing with people and having them see God's truth is like soaring above the Colorado Rockies. When I am used by God through my passion, ministry becomes easy, or natural, and it actually refuels me.

Can you imagine how God might feel as He watches and empowers this process? I think He has a twinkle in His eye and a big smile on His face. I not only experience great enjoyment by walking in my calling, but glory is given to God, and He is thrilled watching me.

Watching my own children and grandchildren doing what they love, with exhilaration on their faces, fills me with joy. However, my joy pales in comparison to the magnitude of enjoyment we give our heavenly Father when we walk in our destiny. As much as God enjoys seeing us fulfilled in all we do, He is still more interested in who we are.

As much as God enjoys seeing us fulfilled in all we do, He is still more interested in who we are.

Dallas Willard says this well: "The most important thing in your life is not what you do; it's who you become. That's what you will take into eternity."[43]

As a mother and grandmother, I see the truth of this. I love seeing all that my children and grandchildren do, but more importantly, I love seeing who they are becoming. Part of the destiny God has for us certainly involves *doing*, but it also involves God's righteousness being formed in us and expressing itself through our *being* as it spills over into how we live our lives and touch others.

Righteous Living

Living in ways that are righteous pleases God and brings abundance into our lives. Still, there is more to our destiny than having an abundant life for our own sakes. We are called to live righteous lives so we will reflect God to the world and be shining testimonies of who He is.

Paul reminds us of this: "The night is almost gone; the day of salvation will soon be here. So remove your dark deeds like dirty clothes, and put on the shining armor of right living. Because we belong to the day, we must live decent lives for all to see" (Romans 13:12–13 NLT).

> **We are called to live righteous lives so we will reflect God to the world and be a shining testimony of who He is.**

It is clear that we are currently living in dark times. Many people are experiencing difficult circumstances in their lives. There is coming a time when Christ will return and bring the fulfillment of God's end-times promises. Until that time, however, we are called to put off all the things that hinder us from shining righteously to the world. This has been the journey we've been walking—getting rid of the old dirty clothes so we can wear our divine shining armor.

Paul's word choice in the Romans 13 passage reminds me of two critical keys to righteous living: choice and action. Inherent in all of Scripture is that we have a choice: obedience or disobedience. We can either choose to do what God says or we can choose not to. No one can make us obey. Not even God will force us to obey, for He will not violate the free will He designed us with. If He did, then our obedience would not be birthed out of our love for God but would be purely robotic.

God is not interested in robots. He is interested in our love, trust, and willingness to understand that He has our future in mind when He asks us to do something. He is looking out for our welfare, our health, our joy, and our fulfillment. Choice and motivation are not only important to us, but they are also important to God. "Choose this day whom you will serve" (Joshua 24:15).

The choice is ours—live righteously or not. We need to know that sometimes the choice will be difficult and will come at a cost. It will invariably mean picking up our own cross daily (Matthew 10:38). Yet God's promise for those who choose Him is blessing and abundance. His life will be formed in them. The Bible makes it clear that we will become enslaved to what we choose to obey. A life of obedience to God and His purpose will lead to righteous living (Romans 6:16).

Years ago, I made my choice, like Joshua, to follow the Lord no matter what. This has not always been easy, but it is well worth it as it has enabled me to actuate my purpose.

The Romans 13 passage also points out that we must act in order to live righteously. In this passage, we are told to both "remove" and "put on." This concept is repeated throughout the Bible, calling us to act in response to what we read. Many actions reflect God's character to the world, such as walking in holiness, demonstrating humility, producing the fruit of the Spirit, living in peace, having love for others, being content, pursuing unity with the brethren, walking in selflessness, displaying compassion, and proclaiming God's truth and love in His authority, to name a few things. My point here is that on your journey to finding your purpose, you will always be called upon to choose and to act. My prayer for each of us is that we would always choose God and act in obedience. This will lead you ever closer to fulfilling your destiny.

There are several other aspects of living righteously. We are called to live in community, and we will rarely fulfill anything of significance apart from others. The Trinity models community to us by revealing each member of the Trinity as unique and as having clear, individualized roles. You cannot separate them and get a full picture of the Divine. Each works in harmony with the others.

We, too, are called to live and function within the body of Christ. We are all unique members of the body serving God together. When we come to Christ, we become part of a whole new family. This family will be there to help us grow and develop, to supply wisdom and direction, and to provide protection from the Enemy. Regrettably, we can be dysfunctional as a family, sometimes falling short of fulfilling our purpose together. Nonetheless, community is how God intends for us to function.

Boundaries, another key concept of living righteously, was difficult for me to understand, but it is critical to walking in destiny. Boundaries protect and promote focus on God's plan, and the concept originates with Him. Do you remember the tree that Adam and Eve weren't to eat from (Genesis 2:17)? This was a God-given boundary used to teach them. Healthy boundaries are a good thing. I grew up without understanding this.

Having been sexually abused, I thought I couldn't say no and so could not set healthy boundaries. When I became a Christian, this lie continued to reverberate in my heart, and I ended up doing a lot of things God didn't sanction. Once I learned that boundaries are healthy (and God's idea), I was more able to tentatively put healthy ones in place.

Let me briefly explain a couple points about boundaries I learned from Drs. Henry Cloud and John Townsend:

- Boundaries serve as property lines, and they help us know what our responsibility is and what it is not.
- The purpose of boundaries is to keep the good in and the bad out, acting as an alarm system and protecting our freedom.[44]

In light of Scripture, boundaries are critical. God uses them to protect us, to keep us safe, and to show us what He desires and expects. If we are going to reclaim our destiny, it is critical for us to pursue God's leading and place necessary boundaries in our lives.

Dave Buehring expresses that boundaries are critical for following God: "What God initiates, He permeates with His presence. What we initiate, we have to sustain by our own efforts."

Placing healthy boundaries makes way for God to permeate our lives.

Placing healthy boundaries makes a way for God to permeate our lives so we won't become pulled in different directions with things, people, or activities that are not part of God's design. Boundaries make a way for God's plan and purpose to unfold in our lives so we aren't distracted by a multitude of other things that are scattered in our paths.

In the end, righteous living boils down to a simple, yet most significant key: our lives are not our own. Our lives were bought with a very steep price—the death of God's beloved Son. When we give our lives to Christ, we are no longer our own. Maybe you have seen the bumper sticker that says, "God is my co-pilot." This idea is erroneous because when you give your heart to Christ, He takes over as the "pilot." He is in charge, and we willingly give our lives to Him.

It is imperative that we fully embrace this key if we want to ultimately reclaim our destiny. Why? Because His plan, His destiny, His way of living, His dreams for our lives, and His purpose are so much greater than we could ever imagine. The God who created mankind, as well as the intricacies of our universe and planets, is for us! He is for you and your highest good. He loves you with an everlasting love that cannot and will not ever fail. This same God is committed to bringing us "up from the ashes" and into His original design and purpose.

God is for you and your highest good.

This God—our God—is worthy of our trust and the surrender of our lives to His plan and purpose.

A Few Last-Minute Thoughts

As we wind down and I leave you to continue your journey, I have a few last-minute thoughts to share. They are simply things to "do" that will allow your destiny to unfold lest you slip into passivity as you journey through life.

In contrast to my previous warning not to be continually busy "doing," I endorse this type of doing, and I assure you that it will enhance your "being" in Christ and discovering your destiny.

Dinah's Dos

1. *Study*: The Bible encourages us to study the Word of God in order to be approved and in order to give an account of our faith to others (2 Timothy 2:15; 4:2). The Word is an essential element for discovering God's original design and purpose. Apart from it, we will be blindly searching for our destiny. The Word can be difficult to understand, but there are many Bible aids and studies to help. I have grown the most in intimacy with God when I have prioritized studying the Word. The Word of God has become God's love letter to me. Through it, He teaches, gives wisdom, reveals Himself, corrects, reproves, counsels, and gives life to me so that I can be equipped to do all He has called me to (2 Timothy 3:16–17). I can't encourage you enough, if you want to fulfill God's purpose, to dig for the treasures He has provided for you in His Word. His Word will be a light to your path that helps you navigate through your life journey (Psalm 119:105).

   The Word is an essential element.

2. *Focus*: With so many things vying for our attention, it takes diligent focus to become the image bearers God intends. The author of Hebrews encourages us to fix our eyes on Jesus (Hebrews 12:2). The

Greek word used for "fix" means "to turn the eyes away from other things and fix them on something."[45] Therefore, although it might require you to establish healthy boundaries, I encourage you to take your focus off anything that is hindering your walk with God and to begin focusing on Jesus. I once saw an object lesson in which a glass jar was used to represent our lives. First, it was filled with large rocks to represent the important things of our lives. Once the large rocks were in the jar, those things in our lives that are not as important, represented by sand, could fill in the gaps. If we instead let the little things fill up our lives, then there is no room for the important things. If you haven't done so already, I would encourage you to ask the Lord to help you evaluate all the things in your life, and then eliminate anything that is hindering your focus on God. Focusing on God is a "big rock" that we need to prioritize in order to fulfill our purpose.

Shift your focus from anything that is hindering you to focus on Jesus.

3. *Think*: My first inductive Bible study was on Philippians. One of the most impactful takeaways I received was a sentence used by the facilitator: "In everything, Philippians 4:8 it." The facilitator referring to the apostle Paul's prescription for thoughts in the book of Philippians is: "Whatever is true, whatever is honorable, whatever is just, whatever is pure, whatever is lovely, whatever is commendable, if there is any excellence, if there is anything worthy of praise, think about these things" (Philippians 4:8). This verse has become my measuring stick for the things I think about and those I shouldn't. It isn't always easy to stay true to this verse; sometimes it's downright difficult. However, as we follow this advice, we are promised that the God of peace will be with us (Philippians 4:9). Philippians 4:8 definitely reminds me to think about more positive things. Maybe it will be a helpful reminder for you too.

4. *Love*: I've been married for forty-two years now, and I can unabashedly say that I am still in love with my husband. I actually love him more today than ever before. Why? Because I know him more, and

the more I know him, the more I love him. I have found this to mirror my relationship with the Lord: the more I know Him, the more I fall in love with Him. Jesus longs for this—a mutual love relationship that never wanes. Revelation 2 exposes the church of Ephesus as a church whose members had lost their first love—their love for Jesus Christ (Revelation 2:4). They weren't experiencing the love for Christ they previously had. Similar to marriage, maintaining our "first love" for God over time isn't easy. It not only requires commitment, but it also requires hard work. I have experienced times where I've been less attentive to the Lord. As I imagine the Ephesian Christians might have done, I became too distracted with other things. Consequently, my life suffered and my reflection of God became dull. If you are feeling this way, I want to encourage you to turn back to Him and embrace the things you've done before that stirred your heart to love (Revelation 2:5).

The more I know Him the more I fall in love with Him.

5. *Lean*: As I journeyed through life with a faulty foundation and mindset, I learned that what I think is not always accurate. I need new insights and perspectives from others who speak into my life. This has been true as well in regard to God. I have come to understand that His way is not my natural way of thinking or behaving. As a result, I have learned to lean more on God than on myself. God promises to make our life path straight if we trust in Him instead of leaning on our own understanding (Proverbs 3:5–6). That is easier said than done. Still, He promises. I have discovered that even if what God says doesn't make sense to me, trusting and following His leading has always worked out for my benefit.

6. *Fast*: As much as I don't like the thought of fasting, I have found it to be a valuable practice. It encourages death to self and openness of spirit, and it allows me to hear more clearly from God. Christ modeled fasting before His temptation in the wilderness. Although His body was weak from forty days of fasting, His spirit remained strong as He battled Satan. The Bible makes it clear that fasting is

not just suggested, but is expected. Christ gave us this instruction: "When you fast . . ." (Matthew 6:16), making His expectation abundantly clear. Therefore, as models of Christ, we are required to adopt the practice of fasting. When God called me to do a twenty-one-day liquid fast, I was in shock, but I obeyed. I was in awe at how God enabled me to fulfill His directive without much difficulty, and I saw God's faithfulness and grace firsthand. Maybe you already practice fasting, but if not, I encourage you to try it. Fasting is an integral part of being formed into Christ's image.

> **The redemptive work of Christ on the cross guarantees we can all have redeemed lives, realigned with God's original purpose.**

As I have opened my life to you, my greatest hope is that God might use my story to engender hope in yours. Many lives have been marred and damaged by the Enemy, who is hell-bent on destruction. Thankfully, that is not the end of the story. Our lives don't need to be irreparably damaged by the experiences we've had. The redemptive work of Christ on the cross guarantees that we can have redeemed lives that are realigned with God's original purpose.

Since you are surrounded by a host of witnesses who have navigated this journey before you, may you lay aside every weight, every faulty foundation, every entrenched mindset, and every sin that clings to you and binds you. I pray that you will have endurance so you can victoriously run the life race that is set before you (see Hebrews 12:1).

As you run with your hand securely held in Christ's, you will ascend up from the ashes and reclaim your destiny. I look forward to seeing all that the Lord does in and through you!

> *The Lord bless you and keep you;*
> *the Lord make his face to shine*
> *upon you and be gracious to you;*
> *the Lord lift up his countenance*
> *upon you and give you peace.*
> Numbers 6:24-25

Resources

BIBLE STUDY

Kay Arthur Bible studies

Gordon D. Fee and Douglas Stuart, *How to Read the Bible for All Its Worth* (Zondervan Academic)

Beth Moore Bible studies

R. C. Sproul, *Knowing Scripture* (IVP Books)

Jen Wilken, *Women of the Word* (Crossway)

HEALING/ DELIVERANCE

Dan B. Allender, *Healing the Wounded Heart* (Baker Books)

Dawna De Silva and Teresa Liebscher, *SOZO* (Destiny Image Publishers)

David Eckman, PhD, *Becoming Who God Intended* (Harvest House Publishers)

John and Stasi Eldredge, *Captivating* (Thomas Nelson)

Leif Hetland, *Healing the Orphan Spirit* (CreateSpace Independent Publishing)

Dr. Caroline Leaf, *Who Switched Off My Brain?* (Switch on Your Brain International LLC)

Francis MacNutt, *Healing* (Ave Maria Press)

Joyce Meyers, *Battlefield of the Mind* (Warner Faith)

J. Keith Miller, *A Hunger for Healing* (HarperOne)

Beth Moore, *Breaking Free* (Lifeway Christian Resources)

Adam Narciso, *New Identity* (Adam Narciso Ministries)

James Robison and Robert Morris, *Living Free: Breaking the Cycle of Defeat* (Life Outreach)

Jennifer Rothschild, *Me, Myself & Lies* (Lifeway Press)

Peter Scazzero, *Emotionally Healthy Leader* (Zondervan)

Peter Scazzero, *Emotionally Healthy Spirituality* (Zondervan)

David A. Seamands, *Healing for Damaged Emotions* (David C. Cook)

Alice Smith, *Beyond the Lie* (Bethany House)

Dan Sneed, *The Power of a New Identity* (Sovereign World Ltd.)

SPIRITUALITY

Paul E. Billheimer, *Destined for the Throne* (Bethany House Publishers)

Henry & Richard Blackaby and Claude V. King, *Experiencing God: Knowing and Doing the Will of God* (Lifeway Press)

David Buehring, *A Discipleship Journey* (Lionshare Publishing)

Graham Cooke, *Being with God Series* (Sovereign World)

Ted Dekker, *The Forgotten Way Meditations* (Outlaw Studios)

John Eldredge, *Beautiful Outlaw* (FaithWords)

Richard J. Foster, *Celebration of Discipline* (HarperOne)

Elizabeth George, *A Woman's Walk with God* (Harvest House Publishers)

Les Hewitt and Dr. Charlie Self, *The Power of Faithful Focus* (Faith Communications)

Benny Hinn, *Good Morning, Holy Spirit* (Thomas Nelson)

Benny Hinn, *Welcome, Holy Spirit* (Thomas Nelson)

Brother Lawrence, *The Practice of the Presence of God* (Whitaker House)

Beth Moore, *Believing God* (Broadman & Holman Publishers)

Kay Warren, *Choose Joy: Because Happiness Isn't Enough* (Revell)

Jen Wilken, *None Like Him* (Crossway)

Jen Wilken, *In His Image* (Crossway)

MISCELLANEOUS

David Buehring, *The Jesus Blueprint* (HigherLife Publishing)

David Buehring, *The Greatest Opportunity* (Morgan James Faith)

Gary Chapman, *The Five Love Languages* (Northfield Publishing)

Resources

Dr. Henry Cloud and Dr. John Townsend, *Boundaries* (Zondervan)

Dr. Henry Cloud and Dr. John Townsend, *Boundaries with Kids* (Zondervan)

Dr. Henry Cloud and Dr. John Townsend, *Boundaries in Marriage* (Zondervan)

Dr. Emerson Eggerichs, *Love & Respect: The Love She Most Desires; The Respect He Desperately Needs* (Thomas Nelson)

W. Phillip Keller, *A Shepherd Looks at Psalm 23* (Zondervan)

Francine Rivers, *Redeeming Love* (Francine Rivers)

Tommy Tenney, *The God Catchers: Experiencing the Manifest Presence of God* (Thomas Nelson)

Tommy Tenney, *The God Chasers: My Soul Follows Hard after Thee* (Destiny Image Publishers)

Endnotes

CHAPTER 1

1 Marion Ingergneri, during her presentation "Legacy Builders," Women in Ministry Leadership Summit, February 9, 2021.

2 *Merriam-Webster's Unabridged Dictionary*, s.v. "refuge," https://unabridged. merriam-webster.com/unabridged/refuge.

CHAPTER 2

3 "The Importance of Foundations," Martin Perry Associates, August 10, 2020, https://mperryassociates.com/blog/importance-foundations/.

4 Dr. Saul McLeod, "Maslow's Hierarchy of Needs," *Simply Psychology* (March 20, 2020), https://www.simplypsychology.org/maslow.html.

CHAPTER 3

5 Mike Riches, *Living Free*, (Gig Harbor, WA: Sycamore Publications, 2011), 8.

6 Brian Brennt and Mike Riches, *Freedom Class Manual: Knowing Christ Intimately, Experiencing Life Abundantly* (Tacoma, WA: City Central Publishing, 2010), 31–32.

7 Elaine Hunter, "'Children Are like Little Sponges': Early Learning Can Set Them Up for Life," *Theirworld*, January 18, 2018, https://theirworld.org/news/early-learning-sets-up-young-children-for-life.

8 Riches, *Living Free*, 10.

9 "Prayer of Salvation," https://www.allaboutgod.com/prayer-of-salvation.htm.

CHAPTER 5

10 Peter Scazzero, *Emotionally Healthy Spirituality* (Grand Rapids: Zondervan, 2006), 53.

11 *Merriam-Webster*, s.v. "mining," https://www.merriam-webster.com/dictionary/mine.

CHAPTER 6

12 Brennt and Riches, *Freedom Class Manual*, 31.

13 Brennt and Riches, *Freedom Class Manual*, 33.

14 Brennt and Riches, *Freedom Class Manual*, 33.

15 Brennt and Riches, *Freedom Class Manual*, 31.

16 Dave Buehring, "Living Free," PowerPoint Slide 8, presentation at informal gathering of a private home, July 2008

17 Merriam-Webster, s.v. "stronghold," https://www.merriam-webster.com/dictionary/stronghold.

18 Brennt and Riches, *Freedom Class Manual*, 17.

19 Quote is used by permission from Randy Young.

20 Alice Smith, *Beyond the Lie* (Bloomington: Bethany House, 2006), 65.

21 Smith, *Beyond the Lie*, 65.

22 Sonia D. Ferencik and Rachel Ramirez-Hammond, Trauma-Informed Care: *Best Practices and Protocols for Ohio's Domestic Violence Programs*, Ohio Domestic Violence Network, 17, http://www.ncdsv.org/images/ODVN_Trauma-InformedCareBestPracticesAndProtocols.pdf.

23 Dan B. Allender, *The Wounded Heart: Hope for Adult Victims of Childhood Sexual Abuse* (Carol Stream, IL: NavPress, 1990), 31–32.

24 Ferencik and Ramirez-Hammond, Trauma-Informed Care, 16.

25 Allender, *The Wounded Heart*, 51.

26 Bessel van der Kolk, *The Body Keeps the Score: Brain, Mind, and Body in the Healing of Trauma* (New York: Penguin Books, 2014), 21.

CHAPTER 7

27 Hannah Hurnard, *Hinds' Feet on High Places* (Carol Stream, IL: Tyndale House Publishers Inc., 1975), 48–49.

28 David A. Seamands, *Healing for Damaged Emotions (*Colorado Springs: Cook Communications Ministries, 2002), 69.

29 Brennt and Riches, *Freedom Class Manual*, 18.

30 Dave Buehring, *A Discipleship Journey: A Proven and Practical Tool for Making Disciples of Jesus.* (Brentwood, TN: Lionshare Publishing, 2021), 9.

31 Dave Buehring, *A Discipleship Journey: A Proven and Practical Tool for Making Disciples of Jesus* (Brentwood, TN: Lionshare Publishing, 2021), 162.

CHAPTER 8

32 *Merriam-Webster*, s.v. "restoration," https://www.merriam-webster.com/dictionary/restoration.

33 Robert Boyd Munger, "My Heart—Christ's Home" (Downers Grove, IL: Intervarsity Press, 1986).

CHAPTER 9

34 Dee Brestin, *Idol Lies: Facing the Truth about Our Deepest Desires* (Brentwood, TN: Worthy Publishing, 2012), 33.

35 Brestin, *Idol Lies*, 24.

36 Brennt and Riches, *Freedom Class Manual*, 25–26.

37 Nelson Mandela, *Inspiring Quotes*, accessed July 16, 2021, https://www.inspiringquotes.com/inspiration/60e4fd568efddc-000821c4de?utmsource=daily&utmmedium=email&utmcampaign=60d-d452163936ed365ba7c58.

38 Graham Cooke, *Crafted Prayer: The Joy of Always Getting Your Prayers Answered* (Santa Barbara, CA: Brilliant Book House, 2003), 9.

39 Martin Luther, *Cyclopedia of Religious Anecdotes*, https://quotecatalog.com/quote/martin-luther-i-have-so-much-MpxPPyp/.

40 Debbie McDaniel, *A Prayer to Put on the Armor of God* (January 24), https://www.crosswalk.com/devotionals/your-daily-prayer/a-prayer-to-put-on-the-armor-of-god-your-daily-prayer-october-17-2016.html.

41 Adapted from Psalm 91.

42 John Maxwell, *Failing Forward* (Nashville: Thomas Nelson, 2007).

CHAPTER 10

43 Dallas Willard, "45 Motivational Dallas Willard Quotes on Success in Life," Overall Motivation, https://www.overallmotivation.com/quotes/dallas-willard-quotes/.

44 Sheryl Baar Moon, *Boundaries Leader's Guide,* adapted to use with the Boundaries DVD (2012), 7. Henry Cloud and John Townsend, *Boundaries: When to Say Yes, How to Say No to Take Control of Your Life* (Nashville: Zondervan, 1992).

45 *Bible Study Tools*, s.v. "fix," https://www.biblestudytools.com/lexicons/greek/kjv/aphorao.html.

ORDER INFORMATION